Get More Money on Your Next Job

25 Proven Strategies for Getting More Money, Better Benefits, & Greater Job Security

Lee E. Miller

D1279594

McGraw-Hill

New York   San Francisco   Washington, D.C.   Auckland   Bogotá
Caracas   Lisbon   London   Madrid   Mexico City   Milan
Montreal   New Delhi   San Juan   Singapore
Sydney   Tokyo   Toronto

Library of Congress Cataloging-in-Publication Data

Miller, Lee E.
    Get more money on your next job : 25 proven strategies for getting
more money, better benefits & greater job security / Lee E. Miller.
        p.   cm.
    Includes index.
    ISBN 0-07-043146-9 (pbk.)
    1. Career changes.   2. Negotiation in business.   3. Labor
contract.   I. Title.
HF5384.M55   1998
650.14—dc21   97-14974
                                                               CIP

McGraw-Hill

A Division of The *McGraw·Hill* Companies

1 2 3 4 5 6 7 8 9 0   FGR/FGR   9 0 2 1 0 9 8 7

ISBN 0-07-043146-9

*The sponsoring editor for this book was Betsy Brown, the editing supervisor
was Penny Linskey, and the production supervisor was Clare B. Stanley. It
was set in Palatino by Victoria Khavkina of McGraw-Hill's Professional Book
Group composition unit.*

Printed and bound by Quebecor/Fairfield

McGraw-Hill books are available at special quantity discounts to use as
premiums and sales promotions, or for use in corporate training programs. For more information, please write to the Director of Special Sales,
McGraw-Hill, 11 West 19th Street, New York, NY 10011. Or contact your
local bookstore.

This book is printed on recycled, acid-free paper containing a
minimum of 50% recycled, de-inked fiber.

I want to dedicate this book to my parents, Rose and Joe Miller, without whose encouragement and support I would not be where I am today; to my children, Alexander, Jessica, and Samantha, who inspire me to do more than I ever thought was possible; and to my wife, Lesley, without whose help and support I could not have written this book.

In addition, I would like to thank, for their contribution to the book, Linda Seale, a human resources executive and career coach; Maxine Hartley, an executive recruiter with Pearl Management L.L.C.; Bob Corno, a financial advisor with The Mason Companies; Ted Pilonero, a human resources consultant with the Joseph Group; my sister, Sara Moe, an executive with Dell Computer; and Vivian Eyre, a human resources and leadership consultant with Eyre & Associates.

Contents

The Ten Commandments of Employment Negotiations

1. Be prepared.
2. Recognize that employment negotiations are unique.
3. Understand your needs and those of your prospective employer.
4. Understand the dynamics of the particular negotiations.
5. Never lie, but use the truth to your advantage.
6. Understand the role that fairness plays in the process.
7. Use uncertainty to your advantage.
8. Be creative.
9. Focus on your goals, not on "winning."
10. Know when to quit bargaining.

The Eleventh Commandment

11. Never forget that employment is an ongoing relationship.

Introduction

This book is for anyone considering changing jobs. In today's world, that includes just about everyone. The techniques described here can be used by anyone: CEOs, salespeople, middle managers, software designers, and first-line supervisors. With mergers, takeovers, downsizing, rightsizing, and plain old-fashioned layoffs, very few of us can expect to retire from the first company that hires us. My father had one employer for most of his working life. I've had five different employers since I graduated from law school. A case in point: I left my former employer, Macy's, after it was purchased in an unfriendly takeover.

I had been a partner in the Washington, DC office of a national law firm and I was about to be transferred to Chicago. For several months I had been working in Chicago each week and returning to Washington on weekends. Under pressure, I reluctantly agreed to the move. A friend of mine who was aware of my situation called to see if I would consider leaving the law firm and going to work for a corporation. He had been contacted about a human resources position with Macy's, a position he thought I would be perfect for. At that time, Macy's was the premier department store chain in the country. Everybody knew Macy's: the world's largest department store, the Thanksgiving Day parade, and the best training program in retail. The job sounded exciting. It was in New York, where I had grown up. So I decided to talk to Macy's.

I flew to New York and met with Dave Brown, the senior vice president for human resources, to whom this position would report. We hit it off instantly. After spending about an hour with him, I met with other executives in the corporate offices. Then I flew back to Washington.

The following week I got a call from Dave's secretary asking me to meet with additional people in the operating divisions. That Friday I flew back to New York. In the morning I was put through a series of interviews. Then I had lunch with Dave. After lunch I met with both the chairman and the president of the company.

By this time, it was obvious that I was being seriously considered for the position. To this point there had been very little talk about the terms of employment. I knew what Macy's wanted to pay in base salary, because I had been told that at the first interview. I had done my own research into the benefit and stock option plans. Since I was aware that certain plans were offered only to senior vice presidents, I had expressed concern about the position being at the vice president level. Other than that, there had been no discussion about salary or benefits.

After my meeting with the chairman, I thought I would be flying home. Instead, Dave called me into his office and offered me the job. He told me how impressed everyone was with me. He went over the compensation package and addressed my concern about the title, explaining that corporate vice presidents were considered to be on the same level as divisional senior vice presidents. Therefore I would receive the same benefits as a divisional senior vice president.

We talked for a while. Dave made some changes to the package in response to issues I raised. Then he excused himself for a few minutes and left. When he returned, he told me he had gone to see the chairman. He said that everyone very much wanted me to join the company. He was hoping that he could go back to the chairman right then and tell him I would be starting in few weeks. To make sure that I felt good about the deal, he offered me something that he knew I was not expecting—a signing bonus.

I didn't know what to do. Dave needed to hear that I really wanted to work for Macy's. He expected an immediate answer. Although I didn't have to give him one, I realized that would not be a good way to start off a relationship with a new boss. I was excited about the job. The compensation package was very fair, but I thought that, with a little more time, there might be room for improvement.

I had been an employment lawyer for eight years. I had negotiated labor contracts with unions and settlements in employment lawsuits; I had advised companies on compensation packages and employment contracts; I had read numerous books on how to negotiate; I even took a course on negotiations when I was at Harvard Law School. Yet negotiating for my own future was different.

Since that time, I have negotiated hundreds of employment agreements. I negotiated employment agreements for Macy's and have done so for a number of other corporate clients as well. I have also negotiated on behalf of executives, ranging from midlevel managers to CEOs. Some of the deals I negotiated resulted in multipage, formal, written contracts dealing with every aspect of the employment relationship. Others were oral agreements confirmed by a simple letter outlining key terms. How a deal is structured and documented depends on a number of factors: the specific circumstances of the negotiations, the particular company, practice in the industry, the level of the position, and the relative bargaining power of the parties.

The purpose of this book is to share with you some of the secrets that I have learned over the years. By the time you have finished reading, you will have learned how to get the best deal possible when changing jobs. You will also have learned how to ensure that you actually get what was agreed to and keep it in the event that your boss leaves or the company is taken over. This book will prepare you to handle every step of the negotiations for a new job, beginning even before the first interview and continuing right through negotiating the final offer. Without having to go to law school or spending years becoming an employment lawyer, you will learn how to develop a negotiating strategy that achieves your personal objectives. You will also learn what to do when your prospective boss is pressing you for an immediate answer to an unexpected offer from the company.

What did I do when Dave gave me that offer? I told him how excited I was about the possibility of coming to work for Macy's. I said if it were up to me alone, he could go back to the chairman right then and let him know that I was accepting the offer. However, since this decision would affect not only me but my family, I said that I needed to talk it over with my wife. It was a true statement, because I would not have taken the job without first discussing it with my family. However, it also served my purposes in the negotiations. Not only did it satisfy Dave's need to know that I was really interested in the job; but it also allowed me the time I needed to consider the offer objectively. Moreover, it kept the negotiations open and allowed me to come back to him to seek any modifications that I needed in order to "convince my wife" that this was the right thing to do.

There are some basic principles which are applicable whenever you are engaged in employment negotiations. (See Principles for Negotiating: The Ten Commandments of Employment Negotiations.) One of the goals of this book is to provide you with an understanding of those principles. However, every negotiation is unique. You need to tailor your approach to accommodate not only your goals but also the needs of your prospective employer. Therefore the book also sets out 25 specific negotiating strategies to get more money, better benefits, and greater job security— strategies which can be highly effective when used in the right situation. The biggest mistake anyone can make is to apply a sound negotiating strategy to the wrong situation.

I learned that lesson very early in my legal career. I had been in Washington a little over a year when I received a call from a client whom I had previously helped successfully negotiate a labor contract. That negotiation was particularly difficult and he was a particularly difficult client. We were faced with four labor contracts covering four different plants, each one expiring one month after the other. We had worked out a strategy that involved locking out the employees at the first plant in order to pressure them into accepting our offer. Once they did, we intended to use their acceptance to get the other plants to agree to the same basic terms. Since the other facilities were still under contract, they could not legally strike to support the workers whom we had locked out. This is one of the few situations where a lockout can be effective. It worked exactly as planned.

After those negotiations I didn't hear from the client for some time. When he called, I assumed that he was calling with a new project for me to work on. Instead, he was calling to tell me that there was something wrong with the advice I had given him during our prior negotiations. He had used the same lockout tactic in negotiations with another union and it had proved to be a disaster. After listening to him describe what occurred, I quickly realized that he had not given any thought to the bargaining situation he was facing. Instead, he had mechanically applied a strategy developed in response to a different situation. Of course it didn't work.

This book will teach you how to analyze various situations you may face during the negotiating process and to determine the best way to approach them. It will show you how to implement your negotiating strategy effectively and when to make adjustments. It will not take the place of the advice of an attorney when a legal question arises, but it will help you develop a strategy to effectuate that advice. Most important, it will teach you how to prevent a prospective employer or recruiter from taking advantage of you.

Principles for Negotiating: The Ten Commandments of Employment Negotiations

Important principles may and must be
inflexible.   ABRAHAM LINCOLN

Taking into consideration those things that make employment negotiations unique, together with the generally applicable negotiating principles which can be modified for use in this context, I have developed a set of basic principles which I refer to as The Ten Commandments of Employment Negotiations. These principles apply in every employment negotiation. They need to be kept in mind when you are using the specific negotiating strategies described in this book.

Commandment 1: Be Prepared

When I was a Boy Scout, they taught us to "be prepared." That is the first rule in employment negotiations. More than in any other type of negotiation, preparation is critical when negotiating the terms of your employment. The more information you have, the more successful you will be. This is so important that I have devoted a full chapter to preparing for employment negotiations. (See Getting Ready to Negotiate.)

Suffice it to say that "Be prepared" is the first commandment because it is the most important single thing you can do to ensure that you get the best deal possible.

Commandment 2: Recognize That Employment Negotiations Are Unique

Employment negotiations are different from other types of negotiations. There are certain negotiating techniques that should not be used even though they are effective in other types of negotiations. Employment negotiations are not a one-shot deal like buying a house or a car. They differ even from ongoing negotiations in which you work out a series of deals with the same people. When the employment negotiations are over, you will have to work with your former "adversary" on a daily basis; more important, your career success may depend on the person with whom you have just finished negotiating. Therefore, even though you want to negotiate the best possible deal, you need to proceed in a way that doesn't tarnish your image. After all, the negotiations are the company's first real view of you as an employee.

By the same token, your future boss will want you to feel good about joining the company, to feel that the terms you have agreed to are fair. Moreover, your boss' goal will be to motivate you to put forth your best effort once you start work. Unlike most other types of negotiations, once an employer has decided that you are the person for the job, the primary concern will not be to negotiate the least expensive compensation package the company can get away with. Rather, the main focus will be on getting you to accept the job. As a result, employment negotiations are unusual in that both sides share that same basic goal.

Commandment 3: Understand Your Needs and Those of Your Prospective Employer

Any employment negotiation is going to involve trade-offs. To be successful in this type of negotiation, you need to examine your own priorities. What is it that you want? Are you comfortable with a low salary and a large equity stake? Do you feel confident that you can meet the requisite criteria to earn a bonus? Are you able to handle dramatic swings in income from year to year? How important is job security to you? How much do you value a Cadillac benefit plan?

Understanding your needs will also help you determine what type of company you want to work for. For example, a family-owned company may be able to offer a competitive salary but may not be willing to offer significant equity to a nonfamily member. On the other hand, a start-up company may not be able to offer market salary, but will typically offer stock or stock options.

Regardless of the type of company you are considering, an employer may not be able to give you exactly what you want. There are numerous institutional constraints on how much a company can pay for a given position or what kinds of benefits it can offer. By understanding what an employer can and cannot do, you can determine what you need to ask for. Moreover, you won't expend significant negotiating capital in order to obtain benefits or other terms which would be given to you as a matter of course.

By understanding your own needs, you can focus on those things that are important to you. From there it is a matter of making trade-offs and being creative in structuring the package to suit your needs. (See Strategy 10—Be Flexible: Consider the Possibilities.) If, for example, you have children about to enter college, deferred compensation or equity may be less important than a signing bonus or a larger salary. On the other hand, if you are free to take risks, you may be willing to accept a lower salary in return for equity.

Understanding what you want and what a company can do within its own organizational and budgetary constraints will enable you to determine what trade-offs are possible in order to maximize what you get. The goal is to obtain the things that are most important to you. This knowledge will also enable you to walk away from a job when a company cannot offer the type of compensation package that suits your needs. Walking away can sometimes be the most important decision you make during the negotiations. (See Strategy 25—Walking Away.)

Commandment 4: Understand the Dynamics of the Particular Negotiations

Sometimes you will have skills or experience for which there is a great demand. Or you may be uniquely equipped to fill a particular need for a company. Hiring someone quickly may be important to the company, and you may be the only qualified candidate to have made it through the interview process. Similarly, if you have been able to defer any significant discussions about compensation until the company has determined that you are the best candidate for the job, your bargaining position will be greatly strengthened, even though other qualified candidates are available. These are enviable positions to be in. On the other hand, you may in fact be one of several candidates the company is considering, any one of whom it would be happy to hire. Under those circumstances, compensation may be the key factor in determining who gets the job. Sizing up the situation and understanding the relative position of each of the parties to the negotiations will help you determine when to press your advantage and when to back off.

Commandment 5: Never Lie, but Use the Truth to Your Advantage

Honesty is important. If you don't share my view that it is wrong to lie, then I hope you can be persuaded that it is ineffective to do so, especially when you are negotiating about your future employment. If you lie during the negotiations, sooner or later you are likely to be caught. Once you are caught lying, you lose all credibility. Even if you don't lose the job, you will be placed at a tremendous disadvantage in the negotiations. More important, your future credibility in the job will be undermined.

On the other hand, total candor will not be rewarded. You should never lie during negotiations, but neither should you simply blurt out everything you know. You are not required to answer any specific question directly unless the answer helps your position. You can determine what you want to say and how you want to say it.

One element of preparation is to understand those areas which may be problematic so you can rehearse how you will handle them when they come up. How you respond to certain questions, including any hesitation on your part, will communicate information. Therefore it is very important to know what you are going to say when difficult issues arise so you can give an answer that serves your strategic purpose and at the same time is truthful.

Commandment 6: Understand the Role That Fairness Plays in the Process

When you buy a car, you are trying to negotiate the lowest possible price, and the dealer is trying to get the highest possible price. Even when a series of transactions is involved, you are still going to try to negotiate the best possible deal, taking into account the ongoing nature of the relationship. In employment negotiations, as in any other negotiations, the candidate's goal is to get as much as possible. However, the employer's goal ordinarily is not to negotiate the least expensive deal, but rather to hire the best candidate for the job. This is almost always true if the negotiator is the person for whom you will actually work, rather than an executive recruiter or someone from the human resources department.

The guiding principle for most employers in determining what they will agree to is fairness. Within the constraints of their budget and organizational structure, employers will usually agree to anything that is fair and reasonable in order to hire someone they want. Appeals to fairness are the most powerful weapon available in employment negotiations. Sometimes such an appeal may even convince an employer of the need to adjust its salary structure or increase the amount of money budgeted for a position.

You should be able to justify every request in terms of fairness. If the cost of living is higher where your going, it is only fair to have your salary increased sufficiently to compensate for the higher cost of living. If interest rates have risen dramatically since you purchased your current house, it is reasonable to ask your future employer to subsidize your home loan. If comparable executives in similar companies are given one percent of the company's stock, you should be treated no differently. Your prospective employer will want you to accept its offer and to feel that you have been treated fairly. Understanding the importance of fairness as a negotiating principle can make the difference between success and failure.

Commandment 7: Use Uncertainty to Your Advantage

The more information you convey to your potential employer about your bottom line, the more likely you are to limit what you get. If an employer is not certain what it will take to recruit you, its initial offer is likely to be close to its best offer. What is offered may even be more than you would have asked for in the first place.

In any negotiation, you should let the other side make the first offer whenever possible. Since potential employers almost always present the initial offer, they will try to determine beforehand what it will take for you to accept the position. Often employers use headhunters to obtain information about your current compensation, benefits, stock plans, and so on. They want to know what you are looking for and if there are any particular issues which might create problems in recruiting you. With that information, they will be able to determine the minimum package they need to offer.

Although potential employers may not offer you as little as they can get away with, if you have divulged too much information they will likely not offer you as much as they might have otherwise. By not disclosing exactly what your compensation package is or exactly what it would take to get you to leave your current job, you will force a potential employer to give you its best offer.

Commandment 8: Be Creative

You may not be able to get everything you want, but you want to be sure to get everything you can. Focus on the value of the total package. Look for different ways to achieve your objectives. Be willing to make tradeoffs to increase the total value of the deal. Limit your "requirements." When you lock yourself into a position, you limit your ability to be creative. The fewer things you must have, the more you will be able to get.

If you are creative, you can package what you want in ways that are acceptable to the company. You will also be able to find creative "trades" that allow you to withdraw requests that might be problematic to the company in return for improvements in areas where the company has more flexibility. By so doing, you can maximize the value of the package that you negotiate.

There are limits, however, to what you can achieve by being creative. In the end, you still must get the company to agree to those elements of the deal that are critical to you. If you are not able to do so, or if you have to give up too much to get what you need, perhaps this is the wrong job for you. However, before you insist on any particular term in your employment package, be sure that it really is essential. Most aspects of any deal are really only compensation in one form or another. As such, their value can be readily ascertained and easily traded for something of equal or greater value. (See Strategy 10—Be Flexible: Consider the Possibilities.) By insisting on a particular term, you may be giving up something of greater value; you may even be giving up your chance to get the job altogether.

Commandment 9: Focus on Your Goals, Not on Winning

Too often in negotiations winning becomes more important than the actual goals that are achieved. This tendency is particularly problematic in employment negotiations. Not only is it important to focus on achieving your goals; it is also important not to make your future boss feel like a loser in the negotiations. Remember that this person will control your future career. You will have gained little by negotiating a good deal if you alienate your future boss in the process.

Commandment 10: Know When to Quit Bargaining

The one sure way to lose everything that you have obtained through your negotiating efforts is to be greedy. There comes a point in every negotiation when you have achieved everything that you could have reasonably expected to achieve. At that point you should thank the person you are dealing with and accept the offer. If you don't recognize when to stop negotiating, you run the risk of having the company decide that it made a mistake by offering you the job in the first place. Most companies will want to treat you fairly and make you happy, but few companies want to hire a prima donna. Being perceived as greedy or unreasonable may cause the deal to fall apart. Even if it does not, you will have done immeasurable harm to your career with your new employer. Irving Younger, a law school professor who taught trial tactics at Harvard, taught us when trying a case, once you have made your points cross-examining a witness: "Stop. Shut up. Sit down." That wisdom applies equally well to negotiating.

This brings us to the eleventh and most important commandment, which cannot be overemphasized.

Commandment 11: Never Forget That Employment Is an Ongoing Relationship

Employment negotiations are the starting point for your career with the company. They set the tone for your employment relationship. Get too little and you are disadvantaged throughout your career; push too hard and you can sour the relationship before it even begins. How you handle the initial negotiations can have an impact, for better or worse, on how successful your tenure with a company will be.

Following the Ten Commandments of Employment Negotiations and employing the negotiating strategies described in this book will enable you to effectively negotiate the terms of your new employment. Once you have done so, you will be able to start your new job confident that you have achieved the best possible result. If you do your job well, there will be opportunities to negotiate further improvements as time goes on.

Getting Ready to Negotiate

*To act effectively we still must have a plan. To
the proverb which says "A journey of a
thousand miles begins with a single step," I
would add "and a road map."*

FLETCHER BYRON

In employment negotiations even more than in other types of negotiations, how successful you are will depend on how well you have prepared. Although preparation is a good idea in most endeavors, it is critical in when you are negotiating. It is the one area in employment negotiations where the applicant can have an advantage over the employer. *Typically, employers do little or nothing to get ready for negotiating with a job candidate once they have decided to make an offer.* Their focus throughout the hiring process is on finding someone who can fill a perceived need. After the company finds the person it wants, its primary goal is to get the candidate to accept the job. The employer wants to encourage that person to begin work quickly. Although the company will likely have given some thought to the general financial parameters for the position, it almost certainly will have spent no time developing a negotiating strategy.

Normally the only actual limits on what a company can offer are those which result from budgetary constraints or organizational structure. Since compensation systems, particularly in small companies, are not rigidly structured, employers generally have a great deal of flexibility in what they can offer. As a practical matter, often the only real constraints on what can be offered come from the company's negotiator not wanting to look foolish.

Thus, provided what an employee is seeking is consistent with budgetary limitations and organizational constraints, a company will agree

12

to almost any arrangement it considers to be reasonable. In fact, if you can convince your future employer that what was budgeted for the position is unreasonable, the company will often be able to find the money elsewhere.

Organizational constraints are a little more difficult to overcome. For example, no matter how reasonable your salary demands are, it will be exceedingly difficult to convince a company to pay you more than it pays your boss. It will be even more difficult to convince your future boss of the need to do so. (Salespeople who work on commission are sometimes an exception to this rule.) However, preparation will enable you to negotiate better terms within those organizational constraints. Sometimes you may even be able to get the company to adjust the organizational structure to accommodate your legitimate needs.

Ordinarily companies do not prepare to negotiate with the people they are recruiting. First they decide what qualifications are required for the position. Then they determine approximately what they are willing to pay for those skills, based on their budget and where the position falls in the corporate hierarchy. If the employer has done any preparation at all, it will be to try to determine the market rate for the position. What information the employer has will ordinarily come from market surveys or from informal contacts with other employers to determine what people in comparable positions are being paid. These comparisons will generally be made, if at all, at the time the company develops a budget for the position.

Preparing to Discuss Your Current Salary

Every potential employer will want to know what you currently earn. Employers and recruiters will inquire about your salary at an early stage in the hiring process. How and when you answer that question becomes very significant to the outcome of the negotiations. Your prospective employer will consider your current salary before determining what to offer. For a position at the same level as your current job, a new employer will typically offer a 10 to 15 percent increase in salary. The increase will be greater if the new position involves a promotion or the company faces an imminent risk of takeover. Similarly, if the job involves relocating to a more expensive part of the country, the offer will normally include a differential to cover the increase in the cost of living. In virtually every instance, however, your current salary will weigh heavily in determining the amount of the offer you receive.

How to answer the question "What are you currently making?" is dealt with in detail later. (See Strategy 1—Making the Most of Your

Current Compensation: Discussing Your Current Salary.) However, obtaining the information necessary to support your salary demands before you begin negotiating is critical to prevent an outcome predetermined by your current salary.

If you were buying a car, wouldn't it be helpful to know the lowest price at which the dealer would be willing to sell the car? With proper preparation you can determine, within a range, what salary the prospective employer should be willing to pay in order to hire you. Once you know what that range is, you should be able to maximize your salary within it. Unless your future employer can be convinced to adjust the salary range upward, the range will serve to limit your salary. To get your prospective employer to rethink the range, you must first understand how an employer determines salary for a particular position.

Let's assume you are the controller for a midsize company. You aspire one day to be chief financial officer. Since the chief financial officer at your company is 45 years old, has been with the company for most of his career, and is not likely to be promoted, you've decided to look for a job at a company which offers greater opportunity for advancement. Another reason you are considering other job possibilities is that your salary has lagged behind that of your peers at other companies because of your employer's weak financial position.

Just as you start to put your résumé together, a headhunter calls to ask if you would be interested in the controller's job for a large computer manufacturer. The company is looking to groom someone to be chief financial officer when the incumbent retires in two years. The recruiter thinks you have the perfect background for the job. You ask what the position pays. She responds: "It depends on the experience of the individual." Then she asks you how much you are currently making. You, of course, avoid giving a direct answer to that question. (See Strategy 1—Making the Most of Your Current Compensation: Discussing Your Current Salary.) Then you immediately begin the task of trying to determine the salary range that would be appropriate for the position.

How Companies Set Salaries

You first need to understand the factors that employers take into account when they set salaries. There are four primary determinants of salary: (1) the job's relative position in the corporate hierarchy, (2) the market rate for the position, (3) the candidate's present salary, and (4) the department's budget.

Where the position fits into the corporate hierarchy defines the outer limits of potential salary. Normally employees will not be paid more than their boss, less than their subordinates, or much differently from their peers. Within those parameters, what job candidates are offered will be influenced most by their current salary. An individual's salary generally ends up playing a critical role for a number of reasons. In the first place, it can be easily ascertained by a potential employer. Its reliability is not subject to challenge, since the candidate has provided the information. Moreover, in the absence of a competing offer, a prospective employer will assume that a job candidate will be happy to improve his or her compensation by an incremental amount. Consequently a candidate's present salary serves as a benchmark against which the reasonableness of the employer's offer will be judged.

An offer can also be influenced by the market rate for similar positions. If you can demonstrate that an offer is below market rates, it is likely to be improved. The best evidence of what your skills can command in the job market is what another company is willing to pay. Most companies will at least match a competing offer if they want to hire someone, provided that offer is within their organizational and budgetary limitations. In the absence of a competing offer, salaries at key competitors and information from general salary surveys can be used to determine the market value for a particular position.

Budget plays a role only to the extent that the company can't afford to, or doesn't want to, pay the market rate. In that case, the candidate will often be compensated in other ways, such as with stock or stock options in lieu of a competitive salary. Alternatively, to accommodate budgetary constraints, a company may accept someone who is willing to work for less than market rate. Candidates may be willing to do so because they are unemployed or because the job constitutes a promotion and they do not have all the qualifications which would ordinarily be required for the position.

What Is the Market Rate for the Job?

You know your current salary. You will find out very early in the hiring process whether the company cannot afford or is unwilling to pay the market rate. Therefore, in order to prepare for negotiations properly, you need to gather information about the company hierarchy and determine the market rate for the position.

Where can you get this information? If the company is a public company, the proxy statement is the best place to start. A proxy statement is a document that is prepared by the company and sent to its shareholders annually, prior to the election of directors. It is required by law to include certain information, including the salary of the five highest-paid employees along with their bonuses, stock, stock options, deferred compensation, and other benefits. The proxy statement will also describe various benefit plans as well as the eligibility requirements for participating in those plans. You can generally obtain a proxy statement and other useful information by contacting the company's investor relations or public affairs department. You can also obtain a copy from the Securities and Exchange Commission, a U.S. government agency in Washington, DC. Proxy statements (Schedule 14A) and other documents that public companies are required to file can also be readily accessed through the EDGAR database, which can be found on the Internet on the Securities and Exchange Commission home page at **http://www.sec.gov/edgarhp.htm.** You can go directly to the filings of the company you are looking for by opening the location in your web browser and adding the company's name at the end of the following string: **http://www.sec.gov/cgi-bin/srch-edgar?** *insert company name.* Because the browser identifies the company by adding words to the search, you must use a Boolean format at the end of the string, connecting each key word in the company name with an**+and+**to identify the organization. For example, Sun Microsystems becomes sun+and+microsystems. Thus the full string to locate Sun Microsystems documents is **http://www.sec.gov/cgi-bin/srch-edgar? sun+and+microsystems.**

Hoover's Handbook of American Business and *Hoover's Handbook of Emerging Companies* also provide valuable information about salaries and stock ownership of key executives. In addition, they identify key competitors for each listed company. Knowing a company's key competitors will enable you to find out about the salary and benefits they offer. That information can be tremendously useful in employment negotiations. For example, if you were negotiating to be the director of marketing at Pepsi, wouldn't you want to know the compensation of the director of marketing at Coca-Cola?

Employees and former employees of the company can also be valuable resources. Current employees can provide you with up-to-date information on salaries, benefits, and the rate of salary increases over the past several years. They can also help you understand the organizational structure of the company. The information you glean from former employees may not be as current, but that shortcoming is often offset by their greater willingness to discuss sensitive issues such as compensation. Even if the information they provide is somewhat out of date, it can be adjusted to reflect estimated salary increases over the years. At the very least, this information will enable you to determine the relative importance of different positions within the organization. Accountants and lawyers can also be valuable sources of information. Although they are ethically prevented from disclosing confidential information about their clients, they may have knowledge about other companies that have had dealings with those clients. If the information doesn't affect a client, they are generally willing to share it with you.

In addition to information on the company's key competitors, there are a number of salary surveys available to help you determine the market value of a particular position. For example, Watson Wyatt Data Services publishes the *Annual Survey of Top Management Positions,* which describes the compensation, broken down by size of the company, of 80 different executive-level positions. It includes information on salary, bonuses, stock option grants, the position's salary in relation to the CEO's salary, reporting relationships, and more. Watson Wyatt also publishes similar surveys covering middle management and supervisory positions. Another useful reference source is the *National Executive Compensation Survey,* which provides compensation information for the top 29 executive positions at companies located in 20 different geographic regions.

There are also a number of computerized databases on the Internet that provide compensation data. The following Worldwide Web sites can be useful sources of compensation information:

Executive Compensation Reports	**http://www.ecronline.com**
C&L (US)-HRA S/RU	**http://www.colybrand.com/hra/hrawww 20.html**

For an additional fee, organizations such as Executive Compensation Reports will do the research for you.

Unless you are being considered for one of the top five jobs in a public company, you are unlikely to find out exactly what the person who previously held the position earned. However, no matter what the level of the position you are seeking, you should be able to develop an estimated salary range by determining the compensation of other executives within the company and at competitive firms.

Using What You Learn to Develop Negotiating Strategies

Once you have determined the likely compensation range for the position, how can you use this information to your advantage? Let's look at how our controller could use the information. Our candidate knows what the chief financial officer, her future boss, is making from looking at the company's proxy statement. From employees and former employees, she has an idea of the approximate salaries of other director-level employees. With that information she can figure out approximately how much the company is willing to pay for the position. Once the chief financial officer offers her a salary at that level, there are only two ways to improve upon it. One way is to convince a prospective boss that those salaries have fallen below market levels and that in order to attract top-quality candidates, he needs to adjust the entire salary range upward, including his own salary. If salary surveys and key competitor data show that the chief financial officer and the controller's position are being undervalued, the candidate can provide this information to her future boss. He can then use the difficulty in recruiting her not only to have the controller's salary adjusted but to improve his own compensation as well. Armed with that ammunition, he will become the strongest proponent within the organization for increasing the controller's salary.

Another way a company can respond when confronted with information that a salary offer is not competitive, without disrupting its whole salary structure, is by increasing the offer in ways that do not affect the organizational structure. For example, the company could agree to pay the new controller a signing bonus or to give her an early performance review.

Let's look at how one of my clients, Jack, used his knowledge of the corporate structure in a similar situation. Jack was vice president of human resources for a division of a Fortune 1000 company. He was being recruited by a competitor, a smaller but more profitable company, to fill a similar position. Historically, the head of human resources at this company had always been a vice president, although the position reported directly to the company's president. After researching the organization, Jack determined that only senior vice presidents were eligible for certain benefits. Among the benefits senior vice presidents received were a company car and participation in a stock option plan. After a job offer was extended, instead of trying to negotiate for additional benefits, Jack indicated that he would love to come to work for the company but that a lateral move, even for more money, did not make any sense in his situation. Since he had experience negotiating leases, he suggested that he take on the additional responsibilities of handling real estate and running the corporate office, with the title of senior vice president of administration. In view of the fact that the human resources position already reported to the president, the title change did not pose any major organizational problems. Because Jack had done his homework and understood the corporate structure, he knew that his compensation package would automatically increase significantly if he was hired at the senior vice president level. *So instead of negotiating the salary, he negotiated the position.* (See Strategy 4—Negotiate the Position, Not the Salary.)

It is also useful to learn whatever you can about the person negotiating on behalf of the company. The negotiator will often be your future boss. Talk to people who know that person. Learn where he or she lives.

Ask about his or her interests. Find out about the person's negotiating style. Then think about how this information might be of use to you during the negotiations. If, for example, the negotiator has a working spouse, that individual is likely to be sympathetic to problems that your spouse will face as result of having to relocate. The more you know about this person, the easier it will be to negotiate.

Another aspect of your preparation is to anticipate issues and rehearse your responses to them. You can always take a break before you respond to any issue being raised for the first time. However, if you have anticipated the issue, you will be more likely to offer a well-thought-out response. Your position will be persuasive because you are prepared; at the same time, it will appear to be a spontaneous reaction. This not only will give you credibility but will highlight the importance of the issue to you. As a result, you may get the issue resolved to your satisfaction then and there. At least you will have positioned yourself well to deal with the issue later on.

You should develop ready responses during your preparation to all the major issues you anticipate will arise. Otherwise, you may weaken your bargaining position by appearing not to be able to respond to a key point being made by the company's negotiator. Politicians use this type of preparation very effectively. For example, during the 1996 presidential campaign Jack Kemp had a standard "stump speech" which hit on all the major themes of his campaign. During the vice presidential debates, whenever a difficult question arose, Kemp went back to that speech, even though it may not have answered the question exactly. The answers were still effective, even to people who had heard them before. To someone who had never heard them, the effect of giving a "spontaneous," articulate, and well-thought-out response to the question was compelling. You want to be able to use your prepared responses in the same way.

To be successful in employment negotiations, you need to understand not only the constraints placed upon the company but also your own priorities. What is it that you want? Are you unhappy in your current job? Would you be comfortable with a low salary and a large equity stake? Do you feel confident that you can meet the criteria required to earn a bonus? Are you able to handle dramatic swings in income from year to year? How significant is job security to you? How much do you value a Cadillac benefit plan? What is the minimum salary you are willing to accept?

Examining your priorities is an important part of your preparation. Once you have determined what they are, it is a good idea to write them down. Ask yourself what is important to you and then ask someone who knows you well the same question. Is it salary, bonus potential, title, job security, stock, severance, freedom to be creative, a supportive boss, access to necessary resources, state-of-the-art equipment, status and perks? Make a list of what your negotiating priorities are and rank them in order of importance. Referring to this list periodically during the negotiations will help keep you focused on your objectives.

Understanding your needs will also help you determine what type of company you want to work for. An emerging company may not be able to offer you market salary but can typically offer stock or stock options. In one deal that I worked on with a start-up company, we were able to overcome the company's cash flow problems by proposing that my client receive a large equity stake because the company could not afford to match his current cash compensation. A satisfactory agreement was reached only after both sides took the time to understand both the objectives of the candidate and the limitations on the company.

In any negotiation there will be trade-offs. If you consider your own priorities in light of the company's needs, you will know when it is possible, for example, to trade off salary for stock ownership. You will also be able to walk away from a job once you determine that the company cannot offer the type of compensation package you want. Again, that can sometimes be the most important decision you make during the negotiations. (See Strategy 25—Walking Away.)

Summary of Key Points

- Before you begin to negotiate, do your homework.
- Get as much information as you can about the company.
- Talk to employees and former employees.
- Find out about the corporate structure.
- Review market data.
- If a move is involved, look at the cost of living in the area.
- Find out what you can about the company's negotiator.
- Try to understand the company's needs.
- Determine your own priorities.

25 Proven Strategies for Getting More Money, Better Benefits, and Greater Job Security

*Success depends on three things: who says it,
what he says, how he says it; of these three
things, what he says is the least important.*
JOHN, VISCOUNT MORLEY OF BLACKBURN

In chess, every move evokes a countermove designed to deny the other side an advantage. In negotiating, particularly in the employment context, if you select the appropriate strategy there are no countermoves. The proper negotiating strategy makes use of the existing dynamics of the situation. As in judo, the right strategy turns your adversary's needs to your advantage.

The principles of negotiating, which I refer to as the Ten Commandments of Employment Negotiations, are general principles that apply in every employment negotiation. They should be kept in mind at every stage of the negotiations. In addition, there are specific techniques and tactics which should be used in certain situations. To make them work, you don't need a lawyer or an agent. All you need is to be able to evaluate the circumstances and determine which strategy or strategies can be properly applied. Will every one of the techniques discussed in this book work in every negotiation? The answer clearly is no. However, if you understand your prospective employer's agenda, you will be surprised at how easily you can identify the appropriate strategies to use.

Depending on the level of the position you are being considered for, the negotiations may take place in a single discussion or over a period of weeks or even months. For many positions you will have only a limited opportunity to negotiate. In that case you will need to get everything you want on the table at once. On the other hand, if the job is at a high enough level or the company wants to recruit you badly enough, the negotiations may take place over a period of time. Under those circumstances timing also becomes important. In a particular negotiation, you may be able to use only one of these strategies. In most negotiations, you will be able to use several. You will have to determine which strategies can be best used under the circumstances.

Selecting which strategies to use and determining when to use them takes planning. If you understand the company's priorities, you can anticipate the issues that are likely to arise during the negotiations. It is important, however, to remain flexible. Whether a particular tactic will be effective often depends on how the negotiations develop. The right strategy will succeed in a given situation because it takes advantage of the negotiating dynamics that exist at the particular moment. Delay too long and you may miss your opportunity. Begin before you have laid the proper foundation and you may not achieve the desired result. Of course, a negotiating strategy will almost always fail if you haven't properly analyzed the situation confronting you.

For example, most employers want the people they hire to feel that they are being treated fairly. At the same time, employers don't want to be taken advantage of. Therefore strategies that rely on a sense of fairness can be used in most employment negotiations. However, you can't appeal to a sense of fairness when a negotiator is so competitive that winning, or at least not appearing to lose, is more important than the outcome of the negotiations. Similarly strategies such as bypassing the negotiator or blaming the lawyers will work only in certain well-defined situations.

The discussion of the strategies that follows should enable you to recognize those situations where either the individuals involved or the negotiating dynamics lend themselves to certain approaches. You will learn not only how to use each of the strategies but also when each can be used to maximum effect. The examples are based on real-life situations, although the names and facts have been disguised to protect the people involved. After you have finished reading this book, not only will you understand how to effectuate a particular strategy; you will also be able to recognize when one is likely to blow up in your face. Then, when the right moment arises during negotiations, you will be able to implement the appropriate strategy to achieve your goals. Properly applying these strategies will enable you to start your new job secure in the knowledge that you obtained the best possible terms.

1

Making the Most of Your Compensation: Discussing Your Current Salary

When you tell the truth, you never have to worry about your lousy memory.

H. JACKSON BROWN

Often I am brought in by a client near the end of negotiations to help resolve a particularly difficult issue or to work out the final details of a contract, the basic terms of which have already been agreed upon. At that point I can usually get the client a little more money or slightly better terms; I can also resolve any outstanding issues or identify problems that haven't been considered. What I can no longer do is help the client get the best possible deal. *The major opportunities to improve an offer usually occur at the start of the negotiations.*

The importance of taking action *before* negotiations begin is brought home to me time and again. I received a call seeking advice from a business acquaintance whom I will call Rick. He related the following story.

Rick had been called by a recruiter at a well-known executive search firm. The recruiter's firm had been retained to find a chief operating officer for a small manufacturing company that had just been purchased by a private investment group. The recruiter described the company as one that had been poorly managed by its prior owner, a large conglomerate, but that had tremendous potential. The investors were looking for an entrepreneur who could bring the company's cost structure into line, market their product aggressively, and prepare the company to go public in a few years. The recruiter wanted Rick to understand that the salary might be a little low, but that he would be given a significant equity position. If the company was successful, his stock would more than compensate him for any loss of salary. After some further discussion about the company, the recruiter asked Rick what his salary was. He responded that "his base salary was $100,000."

Rick's response to the recruiter's question was reflexive. It was the response most people make when they are asked about their salary. It was also the wrong response.The best response is to avoid divulging salary at such an early stage in the process. This may be difficult to do; however, it is not impossible. In order to be able to respond properly to an inquiry about your compensation, you must prepare ahead of time. When this question comes up, as it inevitably will, you need to have a well-thought-out response. You should be comfortable enough with what you are going to say so that there is no hesitation. You can then move quickly to another subject without drawing undue attention to the issue.

Consider the impact of what Rick told the recruiter. A candidate's current salary is the single most important factor an employer will use in determining what to offer. As a rule, if a new job doesn't involve a promotion or a relocation to a higher-cost area, an employer will offer a 10 to 15 percent increase over the employee's current salary. Even when a promotion or relocation is involved, an employer will use current salary as the starting point in deciding what to offer.

From the situation described to him, Rick could expect to be offered a base salary at or slightly below his current salary level, plus a substantial grant of stock or stock options to compensate for the company's inability to increase his salary. Unfortunately for Rick, his salary disclosure enabled the company to offer him the same salary and enough equity, in light of his salary, to make it worthwhile to change jobs. That is exactly what happened.

Rick is an honest guy and a terrific marketer. But he had spent his entire career with one company, and so was not an experienced employment negotiator. Because Rick did not have a strategy for dealing with the predictable question about his current salary, he limited the amount of the offer he received. Fortunately, I was able to help him get some additional options. Even so, if Rick had answered that inquiry differently, he might have been offered a larger salary initially and would still have been able to negotiate an increase in his equity stake.

At some point during the hiring process you will certainly be asked, and will be expected to answer, questions about your salary. You should answer those questions honestly, but not without first having given them careful thought. When responding to questions about your compensation, bear in mind the fifth commandment of employment negotiations: "Never lie, but use the truth to your advantage." Not only is it wrong to lie about your salary; it is a tactical error as well. Your salary can easily be confirmed by your current employer. In fact, you may be asked to provide a copy of your last W-2 form after you are hired. On the other hand, as Rick learned the hard way, complete candor will work to your disadvantage.

Making the Most of Your Current Salary

How can you make the most of your current salary without lying? *The simplest way is to consider the value of your total compensation.* When providing salary information, include not only base salary and bonuses but also benefits such as car allowance, reimbursement for club dues, expense accounts, deferred compensation, stock and stock options, pension benefits, 401(k) plans, company-paid insurance, and so on. If possible, avoid being too precise, at least during the preliminary discussions.

How should Rick have responded? Instead of stating that his base salary was $100,000, he could have countered with something like this:

RECRUITER: What is your current salary, Rick?

RICK: Last year I made approximately $150,000, including my bonus and other perks.

Such a response takes into account not only Rick's $100,000 salary but his bonus of $25,000 and approximately $25,000 worth of stock options, perks, and other benefits. By describing his compensation in this way, Rick is communicating that he takes the fact that he will earn a bonus for granted and considers it to be part of his basic compensation package. Even better, he could have responded that his current compensation is between $150,000 and $175,000, depending on his bonus. Alternatively he could have simply stated that his salary was in the low six figures. Finally, Rick could have tried to deflect the question by asking what the company has budgeted for the position.

By including the value of all the elements of his compensation package, Rick encourages the company to focus on a salary range. At the same time, he takes advantage of the seventh commandment by creating uncertainty as to what he is willing to accept. This forces his prospective employer to carefully consider the value of the job, rather than Rick's current salary, in determining what to offer. In this way the company is encouraged to put forth its best offer. It will no longer be able to determine an appropriate offer simply by adding an amount to Rick's current salary that would seem sufficient to entice him to change jobs. These same techniques work whether your salary is $50,000 or $500,000.

If you are asked specifically about salary and can't avoid the subject, be sure to describe your salary in its most favorable light. As discussed above, treat your bonus as part of your salary. Because your bonus may vary from year to year, it can provide you with a certain amount of flexibility (without being dishonest) in the way you describe your compensation. Moreover, the inherent variability of bonuses allows you additional opportunities to create uncertainty with a prospective employer. For example, if the bonus you earned last year was much larger than what you anticipate receiving this year, be sure that you state your compensation in terms of what you earned last year. If, on the other hand, you expect that this year's bonus will be larger than last year's, discuss what you expect to earn this year. Thus you could say that you are earning $50,000 in base salary and expect to receive a $15,000 bonus this year. If the last time you received a large bonus was several years ago, when you were given $25,000 because of your extraordinary work on a particular deal, you can talk about earning bonuses of between $10,000 and $25,000. Even better, you could describe your bonus as "up to $25,000." You could also talk about the bonus program in general, describing your bonus potential, which is the maximum possible bonus you could earn. Be aware, however, that eventually someone will probably ask about the bonuses you have actually received.

If you are due a bonus or a raise, be sure to include it in the valuation of your current compensation. For example, if you are expecting a $10,000 raise in the next month, you should state that "my base salary will be $60,000 when I receive my performance review next month." The same purpose would be served, and some additional uncertainty created, by changing that slightly and stating that "my base salary will be *at least* $60,000 when I receive my performance review next month." This places your compensation in its most favorable light.

Equally important, the failure to take into consideration an impending raise or bonus in describing your total compensation can seriously disadvantage you at a new job. For example, if a new employer offers you a 15 percent increase in your present salary but you are anticipating a 10 percent raise from your current employer, your actual compensation will not have increased significantly over what you would have earned had you not changed jobs. In fact, it may not actually result in an increase at all if you have to wait more than a year before you are eligible to receive a performance review and possible raise from your new employer. The problem can be exacerbated if your annual bonus is due at the same time as your performance review.

If Your Salary Is Low Because You Have Been with the Same Company for Years

A problem you may encounter if you have been with the same employer for a lengthy period of time is that your salary has not kept up with the market. If your current salary is used in setting the salary at a new job, you will continue to be paid less than you are worth. Under these circumstances it is critical to concentrate the discussion on the market rate for the position, and delay discussing your specific salary for as long as possible. Having information as to what other companies are paying for similar positions will help you highlight the value of the job, as opposed to your current salary. When the time comes to disclose your salary, not only should you make it clear that you know you are being underpaid, but you should also explain the reason without being defensive about it. For example, you might state, "Companies are paying between $50,000 and $75,000 for graphic designers. Although I have been earning only $35,000 at the Cheapo Graphics Company while I have been mastering CAD technology, now that I am fully proficient I expect to be paid the going rate." Whatever the reason for your below-market salary, be prepared to explain why you have been willing to accept it and to demonstrate what other companies are paying for people with your skills.

If You Are Already Earning More Than the New Position Pays

The opposite problem arises if you are currently earning more than the company is contemplating paying for the position. You need to be very careful about how you communicate your salary in that situation. If you describe your compensation in a way that is clearly outside the range for the job, you probably won't be considered further. On the other hand, if you lock yourself into a position early on by saying that the proposed salary is acceptable, you probably will not get an opportunity to significantly increase the compensation at a later stage in the process.

The best way to handle the situation is to defer the discussion of salary until the company has had a chance to understand the value you can bring to the position. If you cannot put it off, describe your salary without being too specific. For example, Rick's compensation could be described as in the "$100,000-plus range" or in the "low six figures." If that doesn't work, simply reverse the techniques we have been discussing. Thus you could mention only your salary without discussing bonuses or anticipated raises until later. Focus on your interest in the content of the job and the long-term opportunities the company offers. Once you have convinced the company that you are the best person for the job, even though you have stated your flexibility in terms of compensation you can still try to negotiate a better offer.

Whatever your particular situation, it is critical that you develop a strategy for answering questions about your salary. These questions will invariably be asked before it is in your best interest to provide that information. If you are not prepared, you will answer reflexively, as Rick did. By doing so you will miss a critical opportunity to improve the offer you receive.

Summary of Negotiating Points

- Try to avoid discussing your current compensation for as long as possible.
- Discuss your total compensation, not just salary.
- Take into account anticipated raises and bonuses.
- Describe your compensation in the most favorable light.
- Never lie.
- Avoid being too specific.
- Create uncertainty.
- Focus on market data if your salary is below the market rate.
- Carefully prepare and rehearse your responses to questions about your salary.

2

Asking for More: You Can't Get It If You Don't Ask

You may be disappointed if you fail, but you are doomed if you don't try.
BEVERLY SILLS

Most people ask for too little when they change jobs. They tend to be flattered by the offer. They are timid about doing anything which might jeopardize it. Often they don't even consider the possibility of asking for anything more. When they are really interested in the job they usually accept it with little, if any, negotiating. Most employers, on the other hand, try to find out exactly what job candidates are earning and offer them just enough more to make it worth their while to change jobs. Imagine that you are not particularly excited about a new job opportunity. Since you don't really care if you actually get the offer, you find it easy to ask for a lot more money. Surprisingly, you may actually get what you ask for.

Why do most people ask for too little? Often they are just afraid they will seem foolish. Many of my clients, at least initially, come to me for advice because they feel uncomfortable with the negotiating process. Most have never negotiated an employment agreement before. Many of them say they don't want to bargain. Often they "just want to make sure that they are not missing anything important." When I suggest that they might want to try to negotiate a better deal, I get mixed reactions. Obviously, some of my clients have come to me for that very purpose. Others don't want to negotiate. However, if I tell them that executives in similar positions usually get this or that additional benefit, they all ask for specifics so they can go back and ask for the benefit. Is this just envy? ("If other CFOs get this, I want it too.") It could be, but I don't think so. Once they know they can ask for the benefit without looking ridiculous, they almost always do. In fact, they may feel that not doing so will make them look foolish, particularly to their peers at other companies.

Why You Should Always Ask for More Than You Expect to Get

The obvious reason to ask for more than you expect is that you just might get what you ask for. Certainly you will get more than if you don't ask at all. More important, asking gives you room to negotiate. By definition, negotiating means compromise. If the person you are dealing with simply agrees to everything you ask for, you are almost certainly asking for much too little. Otherwise, by agreeing to your requests, the other party would risk looking inept to superiors. In most cases, for an agreement to be reached, there has to be some give-and-take. If the first position you put forth is exactly what you want, then either you won't reach agreement or you'll have to take less in the end in order to close the deal.

I began my career as an employment lawyer by negotiating collective-bargaining agreements with unions. It is something I love to do, and I still do it whenever I can. In some industries labor negotiations are conducted by one company negotiating a contract with the union and each of the other companies in the industry going through the exercise of bargaining—only to agree, in the end, on the same basic terms. This is called "pattern bargaining." The automobile industry operates this way. Last year, for example, the United Autoworkers first reached an agreement with Ford before it began to negotiate with Chrysler and General Motors.

As a young labor negotiator, I was told a story that I use whenever I teach a class on negotiating. Although I cannot identify the people involved, I have no doubt it is true. The story involves a company in an industry that engaged in pattern bargaining. Shortly before this particular company began to bargain with the union, a new chief executive officer was appointed. The new CEO had spent years in the industry and knew it very well. Although he had never been required to take part in labor negotiations, he understood that everyone always agreed to the same basic contract. So rather than waste a lot of time going through the motions of bargaining, he decided to go to the table personally at the start of negotiations and tell the union that the company would just agree to the same 50 cents an hour annual increase that the other companies had already agreed to. That way everyone could get back to work without wasting a lot of time. After months of negotiating, in order to get an agreement, the company finally had to give its employees an increase of 55 cents an hour.

The point of this story is that negotiating is a process. The new CEO tried to short-circuit the process and ended up having to pay more as a result. If negotiations are handled properly, there is something therapeutic about the process. Everyone feels that the end result is fair. Even though both sides don't get everything they want, or perhaps because both sides don't get everything they want, the parties walk away feeling that they did the best they could. It is a curious process, but it seems to work reasonably well. By asking for more than what you expect the other side to agree to, you leave yourself room to bargain. This approach will allow you, through the give-and-take of negotiations, to get everything possible and yet have everyone leave feeling satisfied with the final agreement.

Asking for more than you expect to get is a basic negotiating principle. But there is a difference in the context of employment negotiations. When you buy a car, you can initially make an absurdly low offer if you want. In fact, it might not turn out to be as ridiculous as you thought. In any event, this type of bargaining is perfectly acceptable. Any car dealer who thinks you are seriously interested in purchasing a car will find a way to get you to discuss a more realistic price. At worst, you can go to another dealer and make a more reasonable offer the next time.

In employment negotiations you lose credibility if you take an unreasonable position. If your judgment or negotiating skills are brought into question, you run the risk of losing out not only on the specific bargaining point at issue but on the job opportunity altogether. Therefore, in the context of employment negotiations, this strategy is more appropriately labeled "Ask for more but within reason." Ask for everything that you can reasonably justify. This will almost always be more than the employer is willing to agree to, leaving you room to negotiate.

Your preparation should include being able to provide a rationale for any request you might want to make. For example, you might base a request for a higher salary on market data. Similarly, you might ask for a particular benefit, or payment in lieu of that benefit, because you are receiving it from your current employer. Sometimes individual circumstances, such as a very low mortgage rate or the nonrefundability of your child's tuition in private school, may give rise to a specific request. At other times you may be looking to restructure a proposal in a way that is more favorable to you rather than seeking additional benefits. In the case of bonus criteria, for instance, you may want to propose an alternative that is more advantageous to you. Be prepared to show why your proposal makes more sense than what the company initially proposed.

How you frame your requests is also important. Ask for what you want, don't make "demands." It is best to appear reasonable not only in terms of what you ask for but also in how you ask for it. Even if you are one of the rare individuals who is in a position to make demands, that approach is almost never as effective in the long run as bringing the employer around to your point of view. If you truly have sufficient bargaining leverage, you will be able to get what you want without either angering or humiliating the negotiator for the company. Tact is important, since you may have to work with that person later on. If you are negotiating with your future boss, it goes without saying that how you negotiate will affect your career with the company.

Remember, always leave yourself room to negotiate. Most employers won't grant all your requests. In rare instances, a prospective employer won't agree to any. However, as long as you can give a plausible reason for what you are seeking, it is unlikely that the company will hold the mere fact that you asked against you.

Asking for more does not mean that you should attempt to renegotiate every aspect of an offer. That would be a waste of your time, and you would quickly lose credibility. Instead, focus on those areas where you believe the employer has more to give. At the same time, emphasize those areas which are most important to you. Similarly, by raising concerns in a number of different areas you can resolve differences by getting the company to agree on one issue in return for your conceding on another. That is the art of negotiating.

Summary of Negotiating Points

- Don't be afraid to ask for more than you think you can get.
- Leave yourself room to negotiate.
- Be reasonable in what you request.
- Be prepared to justify what you are asking for.
- Remember that how you ask is important.
- Avoid making "demands."

3

Seek and You Shall Find: The Tactical Use of Questions

It is often how the question is framed that
determines the answer that is received.
JUDGE SLOVITER

You have been offered a position with a new company. Happily, everyone has agreed upon most of the terms of employment. You are in the process of negotiating with the vice president of human resources about severance in the event things don't work out. The conversation goes something like this:

YOU: Do you have a severance policy?

VP: No. Not a formal one.

YOU: An informal one?

VP: Yes. One week per year of service.

YOU: In the event that the company is taken over or if for some other reason I lose my job, I think a year would be more appropriate. After all, I am giving up a very secure job and moving my family across the country.

VP: No one ever gets more than six months.

YOU: I really don't feel, with all the corporate restructurings taking place, that I could relocate my family without more security than just six months.

That is a reasonable response. It is possible that the company will agree to give you a larger severance, at least in the event of a takeover. If the company doesn't change its position on this issue, however, you have a problem. You either have to back down and risk losing credibility or call the company's bluff and risk losing the job.

A better approach is to respond with a question. For instance, the last exchange could have been handled this way:

> VP: No one ever gets more than six months.
>
> YOU: No one?

Unless the vice president of human resources answers "No one!" you will probably be able to get a severance package of greater than six months. By forcing the vice president of human resources to admit that some people have received larger severance packages, you have changed the nature of the debate. Instead of arguing about whether it is possible for the company to give you a better severance package, you will now be able to focus on whether your situation merits the same consideration as that of others who received additional severance. Since the vice president of human resources will be reluctant to discuss the specific circumstances of employees who were given more than six months of severance, it is likely that the company will find a way to accommodate you on this issue.

Ask if there are any special compensation programs (bonus plans, stock option plans, deferred-compensation plans) that key executives receive. Determine who is eligible to participate in those plans. If you are not at that level, inquire about lesser programs available to people in positions similar to yours. Find out how many employees are eligible to participate in those plans. If the number of people who participate does not match up with what your prospective employer has been telling you about the importance of your position, simply asking those question may result in your being included in a better plan. If it does not, and you cannot negotiate a more appropriate level for your position, this may not be the right job for you. (See Strategy 25—Walking Away.)

Questions are a very useful tool in negotiations. To begin with, they are generally not threatening. Moreover, most people find it difficult to lie when they are asked a direct question. An evasive response in and of itself provides you with useful information. In addition, most people like to appear knowledgeable and will share a great deal of information if you just ask.

Practical Techniques for Asking Questions

Questions may be designed to elicit information or they may be intended to make a point. How you ask questions is important. Several techniques used by courtroom lawyers can prove very useful in job negotiations.

Silence is one way that lawyers get information when they are questioning witnesses. After the witness answers, rather than ask the next question they simply remain silent and see if the witness will continue talking. This technique works equally well during negotiations. (See Strategy 23—Silence is Golden: When to Let the Other Side Talk.)

Acting as if don't understand something is another way of getting additional information. If you ask lots of questions and look like you need assistance, most people will instinctively want to help. This technique is sometimes referred to as the "Columbo approach," after the TV detective who by acting hopelessly confused was always able to get the criminal to give him the information needed to solve the case. Because you are seeking help, the defenses of the person with whom you are dealing will be lowered. As a result, that individual may unintentionally provide you with valuable information which you can use to help make your case.

When you are negotiating with a prospective employer, you have to be careful with how you use this technique. You should not use it too often. Limit this approach to areas where you would not be expected to be knowledgeable. After all, the company is hiring you because it considers you to be fairly intelligent. You don't want to do anything to undermine that belief.

One of the goals of asking questions during negotiations is to try to keep the negotiator talking. The more he or she talks, the more you will find out. An added benefit is that questions help you develop a relationship with the person with whom you are negotiating. Having a personal relationship with the company's representative is always valuable in the negotiating process, particularly when the issues are difficult. (See Strategy 9—Disagree Without Being Disagreeable: Being Likable as a Negotiating Strategy.) As discussed above, one way to encourage someone to talk is simply to be quiet and listen after you ask a question. To be even more effective, acknowledge your interest in what is being said by looking directly at the speaker after you ask your question and occasionally nod in agreement. (See Strategy 23—Silence is Golden: When to Let the Other Side Talk.)

As illustrated by our first example, another technique lawyers use is to paraphrase what has just been said in question form beginning with "you never" or "you always" or words to that effect. This technique is particularly effective when a company is relying on a policy or practice to deny an otherwise reasonable request. For example:

> NEGOTIATOR: Relocation is governed by our relocation policy.
>
> YOU: The relocation policy controls regardless of the circumstances?
>
> NEGOTIATOR: Except in very unusual circumstances.

Once you have gotten that concession, you are well on your way to making the case that yours is an unusual circumstance. You can then follow up by asking, "under what circumstances have exceptions been granted in the past?"

By encouraging the company negotiator to talk, you increase the likelihood of obtaining information to support your position. Information you receive in this way can provide valuable insights into the company. Moreover, since you received it directly from the company negotiator, it is not subject to challenge.

The use of questions not only provides you with valuable information but also makes the people responding feel that they are working with you, not negotiating against you. After all, when people answer your questions, they are helping you. If you treat the negotiations as an effort to work together to resolve the obstacles which might prevent you from joining the company, you will end up getting the best possible deal. (See Strategy 5—Creating a Win-Win Situation.) In addition, by involving the other side through the question-and-answer process, you will provide an additional impetus for the company representative to want to conclude the negotiations successfully. (See Strategy 8—Creating a Stake in the Outcome.)

Another form of questioning that is useful in employment negotiations is simply to ask why, particularly when you are responding to a statement like "We can't do that" or "That is our policy." When you ask why, you call for a reasoned response. Once you are given a justification, you will be able to argue persuasively that the reason given is inapplicable in this instance.

Finally, if all else fails, you can ask the negotiator what he or she would do in your situation. This approach is often very effective in changing the negotiating dynamics on a particular issue. It frequently causes the other side to try to come up with a solution to the problem, rather than convince you that no problem exists. Since the company negotiator understands what is possible, he or she can usually find an acceptable solution within the framework of what the company can live with.

Throughout the hiring process little things can kill a deal. Recruiting is a lot like courtship. If it isn't handled properly in the early stages, the ardor can quickly wane. When it comes to employment decisions, emotions often play a critical role. Unless seemingly small issues are quickly and satisfactorily resolved, one side or the other may conclude that it has made a mistake. Often deals fall through without the other side ever really knowing why.

I recall one negotiation which I thought was going to break down over a relatively minor issue. However, a well-timed question put the negotiations back on track. I was representing an executive in California who was being recruited by a Connecticut firm. We had worked out all the major issues—salary, bonus, and stock options—to my client's satisfaction. The company had a generous relocation policy which dealt with most of my client's concerns. But it provided for only a 30-day temporary living allowance. My client's daughter was a senior in high school, and he felt he could not move his family until after she graduated. He told the company about this situation and asked to be provided with temporary living expenses for one year until his daughter finished high school. The company insisted that it could not deviate from its relocation policy. Although the company had been very accommodating in every other area, it would not budge on this issue.

In light of the total package, a temporary living allowance, even for a year, was not a lot of money. I tried to convince my client to give in on the issue and to use it as leverage to try to improve other aspects of the deal. (See Strategy 24—How to Win by Conceding.) He wouldn't hear of it: "If the company is going to be so unreasonable about temporary living expenses, this is not where I want to work." Just when I thought the deal was about to collapse, a timely question allowed us to conclude the negotiations successfully.

What was the insightful query that helped us salvage the negotiations? It was simply "Why?" More specifically, I told the company negotiator that I really couldn't understand why we were arguing about the temporary living allowance. It was not that much money in terms of the total package, and in light of my client's particular circumstances, paying for his temporary living expenses for a year while he lived away from his family seemed only fair. The negotiator explained that the reason the relocation policy was written in stone was that the company previously had a bad experience with a senior executive. After receiving temporary living expenses for well over a year, the executive couldn't get his wife to move and returned to his previous employer. Knowing why the negotiator would not agree to a seemingly reasonable request allowed us to resolve the problem relatively easily. We entered into a written agreement that if my client did not move his family to Connecticut at the end of the year, he would repay the amount given to him for temporary living expenses. The negotiator could then modify the relocation policy for my client without the fear of being made to look foolish.

Not every problem can be fixed simply by asking a question. Not every deal can be saved. However, rather than arguing about an issue, sometimes asking the right question can break an impasse. Questions are not adversarial. They can be used to frame the terms of the debate. If your position is sound, questions can be directed in a way that brings the other side around to your point of view. Moreover, the question-and-answer process encourages the parties to work together. It focuses them on finding a mutually acceptable solution. If enough questions are asked, they often provide the insight needed to come to terms.

Summary of Negotiating Points

- Use questions to try to understand the company's positions.
- Encourage the company negotiator to talk.
- Listen to the answers.
- Be quiet after you ask a question.
- Paraphrase what has been said in question form, adding "you always" or "you never" or words to that effect.
- Ask why.
- Use questions to frame issues.
- Use questions when you reach an impasse.
- Ask questions as a way of encouraging the parties to work together to solve problems.

4

Negotiate the Position, Not the Salary

Choose a job you love, and you will never
have to work a day in your life.

CONFUCIUS

You have just finished a series of job interviews with Wetscape Company, the maker of small, portable computers which are rented at resorts, hotels, airports, and bars. The president of the company is very excited about the product and has spent the last hour telling you about its many potential uses. She then offers you the position of vice president of sales, the job that you were interviewing for, at a salary of $100,000. A significant number of stock options are included as part of the compensation package. You respond by stating that you would be happy to take the job but only if you are given a $10,000 annual expense account. How do you think the company's president will react? Even if that request is reasonable, the timing and the manner in which it is being made virtually guarantees that it will not be well received.

Although employment negotiations differ from other types of negotiations, when it comes to salary and benefits employers and employees still have distinctly different interests. Employers may not offer you as little as they can get away with, but neither do they want to pay any more than is reasonably necessary.

There is usually room to maneuver. Yet most people don't negotiate at all when they are offered a new job. They decide whether they want the job and either accept or reject the offer. If they negotiate at all, it is usually to attempt to resolve a particular problem they anticipate. Typically the issues they raise have something to do with their move or their families' needs. Those people who do try to improve the financial terms of the initial offer tend to approach the process as they would any other negotiations. This quickly turns the negotiations into a zero-sum game. Your prospective employer will view the negotiations that way as well, with every dollar the company gives you being treated as one less dollar it has.

Employment negotiations do not have to proceed that way. Consider the negotiations to be more like a courtship than an adversarial process. Bear in mind that once an employer decides to hire someone, its primary goal becomes convincing that person to join the organization. It is to your benefit to avoid turning the recruitment process into a traditional zero-sum negotiation.

By recognizing the different dynamics governing employment negotiations, you can take advantage of the one interest that all applicants and employers share—the job. *Whenever the negotiations become difficult, talk about the position.* If your prospective employer balks at your salary request, discuss your ideas about how you would handle the job. Ask about opportunities to increase market share, improve customer service, or reduce costs. Talking about the job will immediately change the interaction from an antagonistic one to a collaborative one.

Employers are not looking to hire someone whose primary interest in a position is money or benefits. There will always be some other job with a higher salary or better benefits. Employers want someone who is excited about the company and the job that is being filled. If you keep that in mind, you may be able to achieve your objectives of more money and better benefits in ways that your prospective employer will not consider to be at its expense.

Remember my client Jack? He was able to get a better benefit package by convincing his future employer to give him additional job responsibilities and upgrade the position to that of senior vice president. He negotiated the position, not the compensation. Even if he had not been able to get the position title upgraded, and gain the benefit package that went along with the title, the added job responsibilities increased the value of the position. With those additional responsibilities, the employer could afford to pay Jack a higher salary without feeling that it had lost anything.

This technique is particularly effective when the position you are seeking is budgeted for less than you currently earn. Let's say that you see an advertisement in the *Wall Street Journal* for a job which sounds exactly like what you have been looking for. The employer is offering up to $40,000, depending on experience. You have the right background for the position but are currently making $45,000. What should you do? You could forget about the job. Or you could avoid discussing salary until you've convinced the employer not only that you are perfect for the job but also that you can do even more with the position than the company expects. When you negotiate the position, salary will almost always follow.

Whatever the issue, you will be a lot more persuasive with your future employer if you discuss the job rather than your compensation. For example, if you treat your expense account as a perk, what you are able to negotiate will likely depend on the level of your position. On the other hand, if you focus on what you need in order to do your job effectively, the reaction will be entirely different. Instead of asking for a bigger expense account, try channeling the conversation this way:

> YOU: I'm very excited about the possibility of being in charge of sales for your midwestern region. The salary you are offering is very fair. I think we would work very well together. However, I have one concern.
>
> FUTURE BOSS: What's that?
>
> YOU: I have been very effective in my current job because I spend most of my evenings and weekends entertaining clients. I'm concerned that my expense account won't be sufficient for me to continue to be able to do so.
>
> FUTURE BOSS: You don't have to worry about that. We'll make sure you get whatever you need.

When you reach a rough spot in the negotiations, talk about the job. Stress how excited you are about the possibility of working for the company. Try discussing all the things you will be able to do if the position is properly structured. Always bear in mind that it is a lot easier to negotiate the position than it is to directly negotiate an increase in compensation.

Summary of Negotiating Points

- Treat the negotiations as a continuation of the recruitment process.
- Try to enhance job responsibilities and job level.
- Discuss skills and experience that would qualify you for more responsibility.

- When possible, focus on how your request will help you do your job better.
- When the negotiations become difficult, talk about the job.
- If you negotiate the position, salary will follow.

5

Creating a Win-Win Situation

Learn to listen. Opportunity could be
knocking at the door softly.   FRANK TYGER

Traditional bargaining theory is based on an analytical approach that I like to refer to as circle analysis. There are two sets of circles: One set of circles overlaps and one set does not. The circles represent the bargaining parameters of each of the parties to the negotiations.

Identifying Common Interests

Overlapping circles indicate that the parties have mutual interests. An agreement is possible within the area where the circles overlap.

Take, for example, a company that is willing to pay an annual salary of between $20,000 and $30,000 for the position of director of transportation. Assume that the person the company wants to employ is willing to accept the job if the salary is at least $25,000 a year. Using traditional negotiating analysis, we conclude that the candidate will be hired at a starting salary of somewhere between $25,000 and $30,000.

The key to a win-win strategy is to be creative in approaching employment negotiations. Instead of seeking a salary of $30,000, which is the most a candidate could hope for under traditional bargaining the-

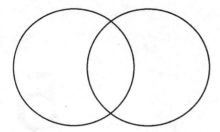

ory, a win-win strategy seeks to determine the circumstances under which the company might be willing to pay more than $30,000. Perhaps the company would agree to pay a base salary of $25,000 plus a bonus of up to $10,000 if certain performance criteria were satisfied.

In the example described above, most people would consider the negotiations to be a complete success if the company agreed to a salary of $30,000. To be a truly successful negotiator, you need to convince the other side to adjust its thinking and improve upon what it initially believed was the maximum amount it could offer. To do that, you have to show that what you are proposing is not only better for you but better for the company as well.

Win-win negotiating calls for a different mindset. It demands creativity. It also requires spending time exploring the other party's needs and desires. Once you understand what the company's objectives are, you can craft proposals that not only satisfy its needs but also work to your advantage.

Remember the employer that would not agree to pay for extended temporary living expenses because a senior executive had abused that policy in the past? (See Strategy 3—Seek and You Shall Find: The Tactical Use of Questions.) Let's assume you were negotiating with that company and were asking for a signing bonus. It is unlikely that a company which has a history of problems with executives leaving after a relatively short time would agree to pay a signing bonus. But it might consider doing so if you agreed to pay back the bonus if you left the company within a year. That would eliminate the company's concern about paying a signing bonus and having you leave shortly thereafter, with the financial loss and embarrassment that would cause. It does nothing, however, to satisfy another company concern: reducing executive turnover.

Once you understand the company's needs, you can propose a win-win solution. Instead of a signing bonus, you could suggest a forgivable loan to be used for the down payment on a house. This type of loan does not have to be paid back if an employee remains with the company for a specified period of time, usually three to five years. The arrangement satisfies your financial objectives. It enables you to buy a home in the area, even encourages you to do so. Unlike the signing bonus, which you could spend any way you wanted, a forgivable home loan benefits the company as well. A home loan allows you to buy a nice house in the neighborhood of your choice. It encourages you to relocate your family. Your spouse and children will quickly become part of the community. Once they have comfortably settled in, it becomes less likely that you will want to disrupt their lives with another move any time soon. The solution also gives you a financial incentive to stay—at least, until the loan is forgiven. This is a win-win solution. It helps the company reduce turnover and the resulting disruption and loss of productivity. At the same time, it provides you with the additional compensation you are seeking.

Creativity is the key to developing win-win solutions. Identify what each party's real interests are and try to find ways to satisfy them. Instead of simply trying to divide up the pie, you are looking for ways to enlarge it. If you succeed in finding a win-win solution, everyone is better off.

Searching Out Real Needs

Let's go back to our circles again. Only this time, you find yourself in a negotiating situation where the circles don't overlap.

For example, you receive an offer from a company you would really like to work for. You are perfect for the job. The company considers you to be the ideal candidate. However, you will accept the job only if the salary is at least $35,000 a year. Unfortunately, the company has budgeted only $30,000 for the position. Under traditional bargaining theory, an agreement is not possible. There is no match between your needs and those of the company. In "circle analysis" terminology, there is no over-

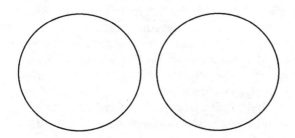

lap. According to this school of thought, you might as well start looking for a different job, because there is no way you will be able to reach an agreement that allows you to accept this one.

Let's assume you are an intuitive negotiator. You want the job and you have not been sufficiently schooled in the art of negotiating to know what is obvious to any good circle analyzer—that you can't get it on terms acceptable to you. Once you find out that the most the company is willing to pay is $30,000, what do you do? You explore what the company's real needs are. You discover that the company is losing sales because orders cannot be filled fast enough and that distribution costs are too high. You can readily identify more than $5000 in cost savings, and by reducing the time it takes to fill orders you should be able to cut the number of canceled orders in half. So you propose accepting a lower base salary than the company initially offered—say, $25,000—plus a bonus based on cost savings and reductions in the number of canceled orders. You calculate that you can earn a $20,000 bonus under the system you are proposing. If you achieve those results, you would be very pleased with the compensation package. The company would also be happy. It gets to hire someone with your experience, something the company did not think it could afford. Moreover, it is able to do so by paying you $5000 less in base salary than was budgeted for the position. If you achieve the results needed to earn the proposed bonus, the company will be glad to pay it. The employer will have solved two major problems and will have increased its profits by much more than your bonus. This is win-win negotiating. By looking at both parties' real interests and finding ways to satisfy them, you have created a deal where, at first glance, none seemed to exist.

Recently I had the opportunity to improve a deal using a similar approach. My client was a marketing executive with a large company. She was negotiating with a small publishing company to become the new chief operating officer. She was eligible for a $50,000 bonus with her current company at the end of the year. (See Strategy 6—Timing Your Departure.) The new company wanted her to start immediately but was not willing to compensate her for the lost bonus. The owners of the company considered their compensation package to be very generous. Basically they were unwilling to pay her any more until she proved herself. So I had my client propose that she be compensated for the lost bonus at the end of her first year only if she achieved certain predetermined goals. The company was willing to accept that proposal because it provided a win-win solution. If she achieved the agreed-upon performance objectives, the company would be glad to pay the additional money because of the increased profit that resulted from her efforts.

Every deal cannot be salvaged by win-win negotiating. If the reason the company will not pay more than $30,000 for the director of transportation job has to do with organizational structure, there may not be any way to solve the problem through win-win negotiating. Once you understand why the company is unwilling to pay more than $30,000, you can at least explore possible ways to overcome the company's concerns. For instance, you might be able to convince the company to place the position at a higher level so you could be paid more money without disrupting the company's salary structure. Perhaps you have certain unique skills and experience that would allow the company to add responsibilities to the job. That solution would satisfy your salary needs by placing the position at a higher level and at the same time satisfy critical business needs of the company. If, however, paying more than $30,000 for the position would require raising the salary of a large number of other executives, it would make no economic sense for the company to increase its offer. No amount of win-win negotiating can change that.

There are two different ways to develop a win-win solution. To employ the strategy effectively, you need to understand the difference between these two approaches. One type of win-win negotiating is based on identifying common interests and developing proposals that benefit both the company and you. As illustrated by the last example, agreeing to a lower base salary in return for the opportunity to earn a generous bonus based on results important to the company is, by definition, a form of win-win negotiating.

The same can be said for accepting stock options in lieu of a portion of your salary if you are joining a start-up company. The company benefits by being able to hire someone it might not have otherwise been able to afford. You benefit if the company does well as a result of your efforts, because the value of those options will rise dramatically. Since the stock options do not increase in value unless the company's stock goes up, you do well only if the company does well. This is the epitome of a win-win negotiating solution.

The second type of win-win negotiating involves identifying benefits which the company can provide at less cost than their value to you. If, for example, you are being recruited to work for a retailer, you might seek a clothing allowance for the purchase of apparel sold by the company. Since the cost to the company for this merchandise is less than what it would cost you to purchase the clothing at retail, it is in your interest as well as the company's to provide some of your compensation in the form of a clothing allowance. Moreover, the company has an interest in its executives using the products it sells. Executives who use the company's products can better relate to its customers. They also become a walking advertisement for those products. In this way everyone benefits. Similarly, a better job title may be very important to you but may not be significant to the company, particularly if it does not involve a more expensive compensation or benefits package. By taking advantage of the different values you each place on various items, you may be able to enhance your total package significantly without dramatically increasing the cost to the company. When this type of discrepancy exists, an "add-on" negotiating strategy is called for. (See Strategy 17—Add-ons: Just One More Thing.)

If you understand win-win negotiating, you will be able to negotiate a better deal. Even if initially it does not appear that the company can satisfy your objectives, you needn't automatically give up on an otherwise good employment situation without first exploring ways to satisfy each party's needs. In one deal that I worked on, where my client was being recruited by a start-up company, we were able to overcome the company's cash flow problem by proposing that the company provide a large equity stake to the client in return for a deferral, for one year, of half his starting salary. A satisfactory agreement was reached only after both sides took the time to understand my client's objectives as well as the limitations on what the company could do.

In every deal you should look for ways to improve your situation by helping the other side improve its own position. That way the negotiations will not be a zero-sum game. The company will have more to give because it will be getting more. This is truly where negotiating becomes an art.

Summary of Negotiating Points

- Identify the company's needs.
- Identify areas of common interest.
- Develop proposals that maximize benefits for the company as well as for you.
- Be creative.
- Explore different options.
- Look for benefits that you value more than they cost your prospective employer.

6

Timing Your Departure

Leave them while you're looking good.
ANITA LOOS
Gentlemen Prefer Blondes

You normally cannot control when the job you want opens up or when a recruiter calls you about an employment opportunity. Moreover, once you have accepted a job, the company will almost always want you to start as soon as possible. Like most people, you will want to begin your new job as soon as you can without leaving your former employer in a bind. Nonetheless, it may not be in your best financial interest to do so. As a result, the start date sometimes becomes an issue in the negotiations.

If there is some flexibility as to the start date, you may be able to time your departure so that you do not lose benefits for which you are about to become eligible. Even if a prospective employer insists on your starting immediately, you may be able to keep the negotiations going long enough to accommodate your scheduling needs. Similarly, most employers will understand that it may take some time to transfer the projects you are working on to others. You may be able to use your need to do so as a reason to delay your departure date so that you do not lose benefits unnecessarily.

The timing of a job change may be significant for a number of reasons. Eligibility for certain benefits often depends on an employee continuing to be employed by the company through a designated date. For example, bonuses, restricted stock, stock options, pensions, and 401(k) plans all typically are contingent on an employee remaining with the company for a specified period of time. For benefits governed by company benefit plans (pension plans, 401(k) plans, and stock option plans) the time period before the employee is given unrestricted ownership of the benefit is referred to as the "vesting period." Rights may vest all at once, as in the case of a pension which becomes fully vested after five years. On the other hand, as is typically the case with stock options and restricted stock, a certain portion of each grant (say, 25 percent) may vest annually.

If you are about to receive your annual bonus, or if grants of restricted stock or stock options will soon vest, you need to take that into consideration when negotiating your compensation at a new job. Certainly leaving a company right before your pension vests may result in a significant financial loss. Moreover, even after you are fully vested, it will cost you money to change jobs immediately prior to being credited with an additional year of service for pension purposes, or shortly before you become eligible for this year's company match in your 401(k) plan.

Most employers will agree to compensate you for the value of any bonuses, stock, or pension benefits lost as a result of changing jobs. Otherwise it would often not make sense for you to take the job. Reimbursement for the loss of benefits is usually relatively easy to negotiate. Requests of this nature are almost always granted. However, in order to be compensated for the loss of these of benefits, you need to know enough to ask. You also need to be able to calculate (or have your accountant calculate) the value of these benefits. Be sure to take into account the impact of not being able to defer payment of taxes on pension or 401(k) benefits and, in the case of stock, of not getting the benefit of the more favorable capital gains tax rate.

Although employers will generally compensate you for lost benefits, they will include the cost of these payments when determining the value of the total package that they are offering. Even though in fairness it shouldn't be considered, money paid to compensate for lost benefits will ordinarily result in less money being available for salary and other benefits. This is particularly true when the problem is resolved, as it typically is, by means of a cash payment at the time of hire. Even if you are told otherwise, your new employer almost certainly has factored these costs into the value of the total package. Any such payments that are made will result in a corresponding reduction in some other elements of the agreement. Thus, for example, if a company is already compensating you for a lost bonus, it is unlikely to agree to give you a signing bonus as well. If it does, you can guarantee that the bonus will be reduced by an amount equal to the amount of the lost benefits the company has already agreed to pay for.

The best strategy therefore is not to have to ask your prospective employer to compensate you for lost benefits at all. Rather, you should try to time your departure so as to minimize the loss of bonuses, stock options, or other benefits. Thus, if you resign shortly after receiving your performance bonus or after this year's portion of your stock option award vests, you will not have to negotiate with your new employer about compensating you for not receiving those items. Instead, you can get the employer to pay you a signing bonus or some other benefit, in addition to what you have already received from your former employer.

Timing Your Start Date to Increase the Value of Your Stock Options

Timing may also be important in terms of the value of any stock options you are granted. Certain types of options, called incentive stock options (ISOs), by law must be priced at the market price on the date that they are granted. Other types of options may have similar restrictions spelled out in the plan under which they are awarded. Thus, for example, a new hire may be granted an option to purchase a certain number of shares of company stock at the market price on the employee's starting day. The stock price on that day is referred to as the "exercise price" or the "strike price." The recipient of the grant will, at some future date, be able to exercise those options and buy that number of shares of stock at the exercise price. If the stock goes up in value, when the options are exercised the employee will be able to purchase the stock for less than the market price. The employee will have an immediate profit equal to the difference between the exercise price and the market price on the day the options are exercised.

Let's assume, for example, that Carla is able to get Small Manufacturing Company to give her options to buy 1000 shares of stock at $5 a share, the price of the stock on the day she begins work. Three years later she exercises those options when Small Manufacturing Company stock is selling for $10 a share. Carla has to pay only $5,000 to exercise those stock options. She can then turn around and sell the stock for $10,000, making an immediate profit of $5000.

Since the "exercise price" is determined by the market price on the day the options are granted, the employee's starting date can have a significant impact on how much those options are ultimately worth. If the price of the company's stock is increasing, the sooner an employee starts work the more valuable those options will be. If the price of the stock falls after the employee begins work, the options may turn out to be worthless. Thus, if the stock market is rising or if you anticipate that the company's stock will increase regardless of overall market trends, it may be in your interest to begin work as soon as possible, even if it means the loss of other benefits. On the other hand, you may be able to rearrange your plans so that the timing of a grant works to your advantage.

During one negotiation I was involved in, the date that stock options were to be granted became a major point of concern. My client had planned to conclude the agreement with his new employer, take a previously scheduled four-week vacation in Europe, and then resign his current employment (with reasonable notice) in order to start the new job. However, my client also wanted to lock in a low option price in a rapidly rising stock market. We were able to get his new employer to agree to allow him to begin his employment immediately and then take his vacation as an employee of the new company. This way he received the benefit of any increase in the value of the stock that occurred while he was away on vacation.

Timing Your Departure to Maximize Pension Benefits

To the extent that you can do so without sacrificing other objectives, try to time your departure so that you maximize the credit you receive for service under your pension plan. Because of the way the pension laws are written, years of service for pension purposes may not be the same as the actual number of years you have been with the company. For purposes of determining the amount of your pension, companies are required by law to credit you with a full year of service in any year that you work 1000 hours or more. Most pension plans are set up on a calendar-year basis. A full-time salaried employee works 1000 hours by the end of June in any given year. Therefore, if your employer has a calendar-year plan, you can get an additional year of pension credit simply by terminating your employment after June 30.

If you have complete control over the timing of your departure, and can do so without losing a bonus or additional stock rights, you may be able to earn an additional year of pension service with your new employer as well. One executive I was advising was able to enhance his pension benefits by controlling the timing of his departure precisely. He left his former employer on July 6, thus receiving an additional year of credit under the employer's plan. This was particularly important, because it gave him the five years of credited service required to vest under that plan. By carefully timing his departure, he was able to avoid losing all his pension benefits.

The executive started work with his new employer the following week, on July 9, and was thus also able to work 1000 hours for his new employer in that same calendar year. As a result, he received an additional year of credited pension service under his new employer's plan as well. Just by properly timing his departure, he gained thousands of dollars in future pension benefits. Moreover, he avoided having to ask his new employer to compensate him for lost benefits. Instead, he was able to negotiate a higher salary and a signing bonus.

You cannot ensure receipt, from your former employer, of every benefit for which you might be eligible simply by controlling the date of your departure. Different benefits will come due at different times during the year. Your bonus may be scheduled for July, whereas the company match on your 401 (k) plan may not be made until December 31. If you get a job offer on December 10, you probably would not want to delay starting your new job until July solely to get your bonus, even if you could. However, you might want to start your new employment after January 1 so that you receive the company match on your 401(k) contributions. An awareness of the importance of timing may result in your getting thousands of dollars worth of benefits that you might otherwise have lost. It may also eliminate the need to ask a prospective employer to compensate you for the loss of those benefits, thus allowing you to obtain additional benefits from your new employer.

Summary of Negotiating Points

- Determine when your bonuses, stock, and other benefits are earned.
- Plan the timing of your departure to maximize receipt of those benefits.
- Ask to be compensated for any benefits you lose because of timing.
- Remember that employers, in valuing the total compensation being offered, will take into account any payments made for lost benefits.
- When planning your departure, keep in mind that for most pension plans you have to work only 1000 hours in a year to get a full year of pension credit.

7
Using the Follow-up Memo as a Negotiating Tool

"The horror of that moment," the King went on, "I shall never never forget!" "You will though," the Queen said, "if you don't make a memorandum of it."

LEWIS CARROLL
Through the Looking Glass

In negotiations of any type, you always want the other side to make the first offer. The reasons are obvious. The other side's first offer may be more than you would have asked for. In that case you are truly fortunate, because you know that a satisfactory agreement can be readily reached. Anything additional that you get during the negotiations is icing on the cake. You don't have to worry about not being able to reach an agreement. You can focus 100 percent of your energies on improving the terms of the deal.

Employment negotiations differ from other types of negotiations in that the other side almost always makes the first offer. If you have been successful in not disclosing too much about your current compensation or what it would take to get you to leave your current job, you are in an excellent position to take advantage of this fact. Even if the employer's initial offer is not acceptable, it is still advantageous to get that first offer. It provides you with information. It commits the company. Most important, it allows you to control the way negotiations proceed. You can select the issues you want to discuss and determine the order in which you bring them up.

To the extent you can control the negotiating agenda, you can determine the direction the negotiation takes. By so doing, you can improve your bargaining position. You can affect the order in which issues are discussed by the way you respond to the employer's initial offer. For example, you could respond to all the elements of the initial offer point by point, or you could begin by addressing one or two selected items, leaving the rest for later. In this manner you can control the negotiations.

Let's assume a company offers you a salary which you feel is too low. You have several options. You could simply ask for a higher salary. Or you could attempt to change the structure of the employer's offer completely and come back with a totally different type of proposal. You might try to restructure the compensation package so that it includes a performance bonus or provides you with equity. You might even propose taking a significantly lower salary if the bonus potential or stock option grant is large enough. We will look at specific responses to particular kinds of proposals in the discussion of other strategies. The point here is that you can control how the negotiations proceed by the way you respond to the employer's proposals. The follow-up memo is an effective tool to do that.

Lawyers have a saying: "Those who control the drafting of the documents control the deal." That is the reason every good employment lawyer wants to be the one who does the drafting. Normally agreements are reached through discussions and are then reduced to writing. Rarely is every detail covered during these discussions. When the terms of the agreement are reduced to writing, the party drafting the document can clarify any points that have been left vague and can incorporate its view as to how points that have not been covered should be resolved. The drafter can also suggest solutions to problems that were identified during the discussions. Once an agreement is reduced to writing, as long as it is consistent with the basic terms that have been agreed upon, it takes on a certain legitimacy just by the fact that it exists. The other side is then left to try to negotiate changes in the language of the document.

In employment negotiations, it is the employer who typically prepares the documents. If there is a formal contract, it is almost always drafted by the company's lawyer. Often the only document that details the terms of the agreement is an offer letter written by the company. It is very difficult for an employee to gain control over the drafting of employment documents. However, by judicious use of the follow-up memo, you can occasionally wrest control of drafting the final documents away from the employer. If a formal contract is not contemplated, you may be able to preempt the employer's offer letter by promptly sending a confirming letter of your own. In it you set forth your understanding of the terms that have been agreed upon and ask your future employer to confirm the agreement by signing and returning a copy of the letter to you.

A particularly effective technique is to send a follow-up memo after each discussion. Following each negotiating session (or as is often the case, each telephone call), immediately fax a memo confirming the points that have been agreed upon. In this way, even if your new employer drafts the final documents, they will have to be consistent with your memos. You thus gain some control over the drafting process.

Follow-up memos can also help you influence how the negotiations proceed. The next conversation after your follow-up memo will almost always focus on that memo, not on the discussion that preceded it. Let's say you have just reached agreement on a salary package which includes a potential bonus equal to 100 percent of base salary. In your confirming memo you could state that you will be calling the next day to discuss bonus criteria. You could even suggest what the criteria should be. Or you might mention other areas that you want to discuss. In either event, you are in control of the negotiating agenda. Since the outcome of the negotiations often will depend on timing, when you raise an issue can be critical. Follow-up memos can be effectively used to implement strategies that depend on timing. (See Strategy 11—Patience, Persistence, and Timing: Outmaneuvering or Outlasting Your Opponent).

A follow-up memo can be particularly effective in responding to an initial proposal, before it is reduced to writing. Let's assume that you just had a conversation with the president of Small Company, which wants to offer you a broader job but can't afford to pay you what you are currently making. After outlining the offer, Small Company president tells you that he will send you a letter setting forth the offer in more detail. You could wait to receive the letter and then address the issues that concern you, or you could seize the initiative and fax this follow-up memo:

Dear Small Company President:

I am very excited about the company and the job opportunity we discussed. I understand why you feel that a company of your size cannot match my base salary. Your description of Small Company's transportation management needs, however, leads me to believe that I can immediately contribute to the company's bottom line. My experience in transportation management with Big Company should enable me to bring about immediate savings in your delivery costs. I am so certain that I can save you money, I would be willing to accept a lower base salary if you could provide a bonus which would be payable only if I reduce your delivery costs. I would suggest a bonus of 10 percent of what I save the company in delivery costs during my first year of employment.

I will call you tomorrow to discuss how we could structure my compensation on the basis of savings to the company. I look forward to talking to you then.

Yours truly,

                               Transportation Manager

Big Company

By sending this follow-up memo before you receive a formal written offer, you transform the dynamics of the negotiations. The president of Small Company has not yet formally committed himself to a proposal. He can accept your suggestion without "losing face." Or he can come up with a proposal of his own that would provide you with the additional compensation you require. Effective use of a follow-up memo will enable you to defuse a potentially difficult situation where each side has staked out a position from which it is hard to retreat. Instead, the follow-up memo provides a way for you to continue your discussion with the president about how to bridge the gap between your current salary and what Small Company can afford. The focus of the discussion is now firmly where you want it to be—on how Small Company can manage to pay you more so that you can join the firm.

The follow-up memo is not merely a means of recording the terms that have been agreed upon. Properly used, it is a strategic tool to control the negotiations and to refocus them when they are not proceeding as planned.

Summary of Negotiating Points

- Maintain control over the negotiating agenda.
- Respond to proposals in ways that shape what will be discussed and in what order.
- Use follow-up memos to set the negotiating agenda.
- Bear in mind that the person who drafts the employment documents can affect the substantive terms of the deal.
- Use follow-up memos to gain control of the drafting process.
- Remember that follow-up memos don't merely record the parties' agreements but can be used as strategic negotiating tools.

8

Creating a Stake in the Outcome

*I consider my ability to arouse enthusiasm
among men the greatest asset I possess.*
CHARLES SCHWAB

Tim had been talking to a well-known New York-based retailer for several months about the possibility of becoming the director of advertising. He was one of several candidates being considered. Finally the company decided to offer him the job. By the time it got around to making the offer, Tim's interest in the position had cooled. In the interim he had been talking to another company about a director's position. So when the salary offer from the retailer was lower than he had expected, Tim said he was disappointed that was the best the company could offer. The company responded that it was limited as to what it could do because of the organization's salary structure, but indicated that there was tremendous opportunity for advancement. Tim repeated that he thought the salary was low and would have to think it over. Tim added that, although he was very interested in the job, he was also talking to another company.

About a week went by when he received a phone call from the company's president, to whom he would be reporting. The president wanted to know what he had decided. Tim again stated how excited he was about the possibility of coming to work for the company. Because of the salary, however, he was having a difficult time making a decision, particularly since the other company he was speaking to was offering significantly more money. Despite the lower salary, he was still seriously considering the offer. He asked for a little more time. Two days later the president called him back and offered him more money. Simply by continuing to talk to the company, which by this time already had a significant stake in the outcome, Tim was able to get the company to substantially increase its offer.

In his book *Bargaining Games,* Keith Murnighan describes a game called the "Dollar Auction" that he uses when he teaches negotiating seminars. In it, people are given the opportunity to bid for a $20 bill. The bidding must increase by at least $1 with each bid. The highest bidder pays whatever is bid and gets the $20 bill.

What makes the game interesting is that the second-highest bidder also pays, forfeiting whatever he or she has bid. The top two bidders each pay, but only the highest bidder receives anything for the effort. Invariably the same thing happens every time this game is played. The bidding starts at $1 and rapidly goes up $2, $3, $4 until the bid is over $10. By $15 there are usually just two bidders and the bidding slows down. Then one of the bidders gets cute and decides to jump the bidding to $19. That person sits back, feeling quite proud of his or her negotiating brilliance. Without fail, however, after a brief pause the remaining bidder goes to $20.

This creates a dilemma for the $19 bidder. The bidder can quit, in which case he or she loses $19, or the bidder can go to $21. Almost every time $21 will be bid. Then the battle begins. The bidding continues to $30, $40, $50. Each party tries to scare the other into quitting. The bidding typically exceeds $50 and occasionally exceeds $100.

Why would anyone pay $100 for a $20 bill? What is really going on here? At first the dynamics of the situation are about the money and the game. At some point the objective changes to trying to protect the money you have already committed. Thus, when you bid $21, you will lose only $1 ($21 minus the $20 you win) rather than the $19 you lose as the second-place finisher. Eventually it's no longer about money or even winning the game; it's about not looking foolish.

When you are negotiating about your future employment, you want the other party to develop a personal stake in getting you to accept the offer. This is sometimes referred to as gaining "commitment." As in the "Dollar Auction," the commitment of the company negotiator tends to increase as the negotiations proceed. A person's stake in ensuring a successful outcome increases geometrically with the amount of time and effort invested in the process. This phenomenon of "escalating commitment" reflects the basic human tendency of not wanting to admit to a mistake. In order to justify previous commitments of time or money, people often go to extraordinary lengths to avoid letting a project fail, even when it would make economic sense to abandon the project. Why? To avoid looking foolish.

The concept of escalating commitment often comes into play during employment negotiations. An employer may become committed to hiring you without any conscious effort on your part. This will work to your advantage, even though you are unaware of what is occurring. If you understand how to gain an employer's commitment, or to recognize when this has occurred, you will be able to use that knowledge to your advantage.

Simply by keeping the negotiations going for an extended period of time, up to the point where you begin to look unreasonable, you increase the likelihood of the negotiations concluding favorably. A company that has spent a significant amount of time and effort negotiating a deal becomes committed to completing it successfully. Once that occurs, the company becomes increasingly willing to compromise in order to complete the deal.

As time goes on, the company will grow impatient to conclude the negotiations and may even become concerned that you won't accept the offer. As a result, it will increase its effort to satisfy your needs. A friend of mine describes how this phenomenon worked for her when she was being recruited as senior vice president of human resources for a major New York advertising agency. When the company offered her the position, she raised a number of issues. She asked about parking, car allowance, club dues, and so on. These discussions took place over the course of several days. The company agreed to some of her requests but could not agree to others. One day she got a call from the chairman of the company, who offered her a substantially higher salary than had originally been proposed. Obviously, the company was committed to hiring her and had become concerned that she might not accept the job. So the chairman made her an offer that he knew she could not turn down.

Although employment negotiations usually are completed in a matter of days or at most weeks, time tends to work in your favor. That is because the negotiator has a stake in not looking foolish for having wasted a substantial amount of time and effort trying unsuccessfully to put the deal together.

On the other hand, you can overplay the waiting game. If the negotiations go on for too long, the company will begin to wonder whether it made a mistake in extending you the offer. After all, one reason the company was interested in you in first place was that you seemed so excited about the job. So it is important that you do not give the appearance of delaying, even though you are in fact controlling the pace of the negotiations. Of course, throughout the process you should continually reassure your potential employer that you really are excited about the job.

One way to build commitment, and control the pace of the negotiations, is to tackle some of the easy issues first. Once issues have been raised and resolved, the other party starts to gain a stake in ensuring a successful outcome. In resolving the easy issues, you begin to build a relationship that can carry over to negotiating the more difficult ones. Another way to get the negotiator to make an investment in the process is to ask questions which will take the company time and effort to answer. You can also ask for time to "think things over" before you respond.

Another way to extend the negotiations is to defer an issue while you seek advice from your lawyer or accountant. (See Strategy 16—Blaming the Lawyers, Accountants, and Others.) This tactic works particularly well when you are dealing with technical issues, such as an agreement not to compete. An added advantage is that as a result you will be able to take a more informed position on the issue when you do finally discuss it. In fact, most people do need advice on technical employment issues. While the discussions about these subjects are being postponed, you can attempt to resolve the issues you want to address first.

If the selection and recruitment process has taken a long time, the employer already has developed a level of commitment to hiring you. You can increase that commitment during the course of the negotiations. Your future boss strengthens her commitment, for example, when she tells others in the organization about you. Whether she recognizes it or not, by so doing she has placed her credibility on the line. She will not want to look bad in the eyes of her boss or her peers. After that emotional bridge is crossed, she will do everything possible to get you to accept the offer. If you are aware of these psychological dynamics, you are much more likely to get what you want.

Once your future boss is committed to hiring you, any additional benefits or increases in compensation needed to achieve that result will seem less significant. The more public the commitment, the more important it is for you to accept the offer. Once an employer has a stake in the outcome, it becomes easier to get small concessions—improve the package a little here, add a little more money there—in order to complete the deal.

Summary of Negotiating Points

- Devoting time and energy to the negotiating process leads an employer to develop a psychological commitment to ensuring its success. Encourage that commitment.

- Control the pace and agenda of the negotiations.
- Try to have a number of meetings and discussions with the company's negotiator.
- When appropriate, take time to seek the advice of your lawyer or accountant.
- Use time to your advantage.
- Continually reassure your prospective employer of your interest in the job.
- Recognize when an employer has become committed.
- Take advantage of a clear commitment to promptly conclude the agreement.

9

Disagree Without Being Disagreeable: Being Likable as a Negotiating Strategy

If you argue and rankle and contradict, you may achieve a temporary victory—sometimes; but it will be an empty victory because you will never get your opponent's good will.
BENJAMIN FRANKLIN

After Macy's filed for bankruptcy in 1992, it was forced to lay off a large number of employees. The company even hired someone from outside to handle the terminations in the corporate offices. Management understood that it would be difficult for insiders to carry out the terminations, because these people were friends and colleagues. The person who was brought in to handle the dismissals had no such reservations. She quickly dispatched the employees who were no longer considered essential and provided them with a standard severance package. Some people tried to negotiate a better severance package but without much success. One employee bypassed this individual and went directly to the senior vice president of human resources, whom she had known for years, to discuss her dismissal. (See Strategy 21—Bypass the Negotiator (Unless It's Your Future Boss). She accepted the firing graciously and asked only that, in light of the number of years she had worked for the company, the amount of the severance be increased. She appealed to the senior vice president as a friend and reminded him that she had one child in college and another about to start. That request was granted. The head of human resources, because of his relationship with the severed employee, could not say no.

Personalize the Issues

It is never easy to fire someone, but it's a lot easier if you don't know the person. Then it's just a matter of looking at the needs of the company. As they say, "It's nothing personal." Not so when you know the person. It's much harder if you have met the spouse and children, gone out for drinks, and worked closely together. The same is true when you are hiring someone. The more you like the candidate, the harder it will be to refuse to agree to reasonable requests made during the negotiations. Accordingly, one of your objectives as a job candidate should be to get the company negotiator to like you.

How do you do that? Think about all the people you like to spend time with. What characteristics do they share? Most people cite qualities like being witty, charming, talented, successful, smart, attractive, and well informed. Of course, these are the qualities of people we see on television and in the movies, people whom we wish we could have as friends. (Actually it is the characters they play whom we really want as our friends.) I don't know about you, but I scarcely count Sean Connery, Meryl Streep, Sharon Stone, and Will Smith among my friends. In real life, the qualities that most of us are attracted to in friends are enthusiasm, a sense of humor, and genuine affection. The third quality is the most important. We all tend to like people who like us and make us feel important.

It is much harder to say no to someone you like than to someone you don't really know. Therefore part of your negotiating strategy should be to get to know the company's negotiator on a personal basis and to let that person get to know you. One way to do so is to ask lots of questions, not only about the issues you are discussing but also about the company and about the negotiator's job. Talk about things other than the negotiations. Show an interest in the negotiator as a person as well. What does he like? Where does she live? Does she have a family? Try to identify common interests. Talk about your kids. Talk about her kids. Talk about golf. Anything the negotiator is excited about is probably a good topic to discuss. It is only common sense, however, to avoid topics such as politics and religion, which can evoke strong emotional reactions.

Although being likable probably helps in every type of negotiations, it is particularly beneficial in employment negotiations. Your future employer will want you to feel good about joining the company. This is particularly true if you are bargaining with your future boss. She has a personal stake in ensuring that you are satisfied with the outcome of the negotiations. Your boss wants you to start work excited about the job and feeling good about the way you have been treated by the company. The more your future boss likes you, the more she is going to want you to accept the job and the harder she will try to make you happy. Being likable makes it that much more difficult for a prospective employer to refuse reasonable requests that you make during the negotiations.

Try to personalize the issues being discussed. If the job requires you to move, ask the negotiator about his experiences when he moved to the area. Seek advice. Not only will the negotiator be flattered but he is likely to provide you with valuable information. Your inquiry will also make it easier to get additional relocation benefits when you subsequently discuss the terms of the move. By using this approach, you are more likely to get the negotiator to relate to the problems you face.

Remember the traits people look for when choosing friends? The same qualities that make you desirable as a friend make you an attractive candidate for employment. When choosing among otherwise qualified applicants, managers want to hire people who like them and who are excited about the company. A sense of humor never hurts either.

Not everyone can be funny, but you certainly can demonstrate that you like the people you are dealing with. All it takes is a little effort to show excitement about the company and the job. Whenever possible, demonstrate your enthusiasm and interest. That is good advice when you are trying to get a job offer. It is no less important when you are negotiating the terms of that offer. Emerson once said: "Nothing great was ever achieved without enthusiasm." Successful executives instinctively know this. The one quality most hiring executives look for in candidates is enthusiasm. Make it work for you.

Suppose, for example, that you are interviewing in New York City, an area with a high cost of living, and you don't feel the salary being offered is sufficient. You could tell the company's negotiator that the offer just isn't good enough. Or you could say that you are really excited about the job but have some concerns about the cost of living in New York, since you are coming from Bentonville, Arkansas. By using the latter approach, you focus everyone's attention on resolving a legitimate concern, not on the fact that it will cost the company more money to do so. This approach takes advantage of the employer's general desire to be fair. (See Commandment 6: Understand the Role That Fairness Plays in the Process.)

Chapter Nine

Avoid Ultimatums

To be likable, avoid being adversarial and never box the other side into a corner. Nobody likes a bully. As a rule, ultimatums are not effective. They certainly won't endear you to whomever you are negotiating with. Even if you have the bargaining power to force the other side to capitulate in the face of an ultimatum, there is rarely a need to do so. If your bargaining position is strong, you can get what you want, within reason, by simply maintaining a firm stance.

If you decide to extend an ultimatum, at least don't make it to sound like one. Which of the following approaches do you think will be more effective?

1. "If you don't increase the salary being offered by $25,000 you can forget about the deal."

2. "I would really like to work for you, but it would not make sense for me to change jobs unless the company could provide me with a substantial increase in salary, which I figure is about $25,000."

When you use your bargaining power in a way that embarrasses the other party, that person will insist on "winning" on some other issue. People have a basic need for fairness or a desire to even the score. They may do it subtly, in a way you are not even aware of. If you are dealing with the vice president of human resources, for instance, at some future date that individual may tip the balance in favor of promoting someone else instead of you. You never know if the person you are bargaining with will be in a position down the road to help you or to cause you problems.

I am reminded of a man I worked with when I started out as a lawyer. We were both associates at the same firm and he obviously felt we were competing for a limited number of partnership opportunities. So he did what he could to improve his position at my expense and the expense of the other associates at our level. In the end, he left the firm and I became a partner. Years later, when I was at Macy's, I bumped into him again. He was now a partner at another firm. He asked me to introduce him to the appropriate people at Macy's so that he could make a pitch to do some of the company's legal work. Somehow I never was able to find the time to do that for him. There is a saying in Hollywood: "Be careful how you treat people on your way up because you will certainly see the same people on the way down." You would do well to adopt a similar philosophy in business.

One of your objectives in any employment negotiations is to develop a relationship with the negotiator. Try to connect on a personal level.

Don't be afraid to express your feelings about how the negotiations are going. You can even allow yourself to show some emotion, thereby encouraging the company negotiator to discuss his or her feelings as well. As long as you do not engage in a personal attack, this type of exchange should create a mutual bond which can help facilitate the negotiations. For example, if you are meeting resistance on a particular point that's important to you, try telling the company negotiator:

> I really want to come to work here, but I am a little disappointed in the company's response on this point. I don't feel that the company's management understands how important this issue is to me. Maybe you could find a way to convey my feelings to them.

Describing how you feel about an issue personalizes it. Once you have done that, it becomes difficult for the negotiator not to try to accommodate your request.

Negotiators generally prize "winning," but in employment negotiations it is more important that the people being hired feel that they have been well treated. Most employers seek to do what's fair. When negotiating terms of employment, the people you are dealing with usually are employers first and negotiators second. That is why employment negotiations are different from other types of negotiations.

Keep the Tone Positive

Try to keep the tone of the discussions positive. It is generally better to say yes than no. For instance, if you concur with some elements of a proposal but can't agree to everything, emphasize the areas of agreement. As previously discussed, it is also ordinarily best to start with the easy issues. (See Strategy 8—Creating a Stake in the Outcome.) Ready agreement will enable you to develop a relationship with the company's negotiator before the discussions get heated. The goodwill that is generated during the early stages of the negotiations will serve you well when you have to resolve the inevitable points of real contention.

Being likable doesn't, however, mean being weak or giving in just to avoid an argument. Never be apologetic about what you are seeking, unless you are asking for something at the behest of someone else. (See Strategy 16—Blaming the Lawyers, Accountants, and Others.) After all, if you can't justify the positions you are taking, you shouldn't be taking them in the first place. Don't be afraid to stand up for what you believe is right. If you do that in a nonadversarial way, you gain the respect of the people you are dealing with. Just keep in mind that very few issues arise during employment negotiations that involve matters of principle. Most issues are economic. Those interests can be satisfied in a variety of ways. (See Strategy 10—Be Flexible: Consider the Possibilities.)

Employment negotiations are no place for Rambo-style negotiating tactics, at least not by you. (See Strategy 16—Blaming the Lawyers, Accountants, and Others.) Nonetheless, disagreements are part of the negotiating process. Therefore how you disagree is important. I recommend the following rules of negotiating etiquette:

1. Try to separate the person from the issues so that the disagreements don't get personal.

2. Always show respect for the other person even when you are disagreeing.

3. Never interrupt, no matter how wrong the other person is. Let the negotiator have a say.

4. Avoid unnecessary confrontation.

5. Argue your position rather than attack the company's. Attacking the negotiator's position will only force an instinctive defense.

6. Acknowledge that you understand why the negotiator is taking a position even while you disagree with it.

7. Explain your reasons for disagreeing and why you are asking for what you want.

8. Present facts to support your position.

Remember, your objective is not to win debating points. It is to get the company to agree. To do that, you first need to get the company's negotiator to look at things from your point of view.

Have you ever been in an argument with someone who refuses to fight back? It is very hard to continue to argue. Soon you feel very foolish. You disarm your adversaries by acknowledging their position. It is completely unexpected. They automatically feel the need to respond in kind. For example, if your future boss tells you that the most the company can pay you is $60,000 because paying more would have an impact on others in the organization, indicate that you recognize how that might be a problem. Acknowledging those concerns does not mean accepting a lower salary than you feel is appropriate. It merely sets the stage for you to begin exploring how to resolve the problem.

Few offers are ever withdrawn because of the substance of the negotiating positions that are taken. However, I do know of a number that were withdrawn because of the way those positions were taken. One negotiation that stands out in my mind involved a high-level executive being recruited by Macy's. I was negotiating the terms of employment with him. Throughout our discussions, it was "I have to have this" and "I absolutely will not agree to that." Everything was an ultimatum. After about a week of this, I sat down with my boss and described where we were in our discussions. His response was "You know I really did not like him that much anyway. Why don't you just tell him its not going to work out?" I certainly made no effort to convince my boss otherwise. The funny thing is that had the candidate approached the negotiations differently, the company probably would have agreed to most of what he was asking for. Remember, nobody wants to work with a jerk. Obnoxious negotiators not only are going to find themselves getting less, but may very well find themselves getting nothing at all.

In the end, you and the company negotiator should have, at the very least, developed a mutual respect for each other if not a genuine friendship. Not only will developing a positive relationship improve the outcome of the negotiations for you; it will also serve you well in your new position later on. That goes without saying if you are negotiating with your new boss. However, even if you are negotiating with someone else, what that person thinks of you may have a direct impact on your career. Moreover, if you have developed a good relationship with that person, you will have created a potential ally for the future. If this strategy accomplishes nothing else, that in and of itself would be worthwhile. Being likable will usually yield dividends in the employment package you are able to negotiate as well.

Summary of Negotiating Points

- Remember that it's a lot harder to say no to someone you like.
- Get to know the company's negotiator.
- Ask questions.
- Personalize the negotiations.
- Disagree without being disagreeable.
- Show respect for the person you are negotiating with.
- Separate the person from the issues.
- Build trust.
- Develop a relationship.

10

Be Flexible: Consider the Possibilities

When you can't change the direction of the wind adjust your sails.   H. JACKSON BROWN

Which is better—a signing bonus or a grant of restricted stock? Your answer will depend on how you assess the company's prospects. It will also depend on your financial situation and personal preferences. Your answer might change, however, if the company increased the amount of stock it was willing to offer.

Employment negotiations typically involve many different issues— salary, stock options, bonuses, title, benefits, and perks. In this context, much of what constitutes the art of negotiating is recognizing opportunities to improve upon what is being proposed by offering to trade one item for a different one. For a variety of reasons, a company may be more willing to provide compensation in one form rather than another. One employer may favor providing incentives to its employees by granting stock options, whereas a different company may use performance bonuses.

Start-up companies usually cannot afford to pay large salaries but are often willing to give stock options to employees at various levels. Large public companies, such as AT&T and IBM, generally pay higher salaries and provide greater job security (although less today than in the past). However, they cannot provide the large equity stakes that smaller technology companies routinely offer. Wall Street firms typically award large year-end bonuses, often more than an employee's base salary. Sales-oriented companies, on the other hand, like to pay their employees on a commission basis. A company's preference for certain methods of compensating executives may be the result of time-honored practices, organizational structure, custom in the industry, or the company's financial needs at a given point in time. Determining what those preferences are will enable you to craft a compensation package that maximizes the benefits you receive.

After researching a prospective employer, you should have some understanding of the types of compensation the company typically provides to various employees. In developing your negotiating strategy, you may want to start with a contrarian approach. That is, suggest a form of compensation or a benefit that the company may find difficult to provide. For example, if the company does not usually give signing bonuses, you may want to ask for one, particularly when you have a plausible reason for doing so. If you have to relocate, you might base your request on the need for a down payment on a new house. Any such request should be made in a manner which is not threatening and which makes clear that your accepting the job does not depend on it. Usually it is safe simply to inquire if the company would consider providing the benefit in question.

This strategy also works well if you are currently receiving the benefit being requested or if other companies typically provide it. Although asking for something that the company is unlikely to agree to may seem counterproductive, it virtually assures that there will be a discussion about various compensation options. You will then have a chance to explore what is possible.

Your purpose is to listen. If you listen carefully, you will likely be provided with important information. You will learn about the company's compensation philosophy, if one exists. You are also likely to receive signals as to where there may be room to improve the compensation package.

The company negotiator may directly address the problem you raise by suggesting, for example, the possibility of a no-interest home loan. Perhaps you will be told that the company has an arrangement with a bank to provide employees with home loans at preferential rates. More likely, the negotiator will focus on the package that is being offered. If the discussion turns to the stock options you are being given, explore the possibility of getting more. If the emphasis is on your annual bonus, discuss the criteria used to determine the amount of that bonus. Ask about the target and maximum bonus. Find out if bonuses are determined by a set formula or if it is possible to make individual arrangements. If you discover that the only way you can substantially enlarge your bonus is by increasing your base salary, focus your efforts on doing that. If the company is unwilling to pay you more money up front, perhaps it will agree to a salary review after six months and again after you have been employed for a year. Listen carefully and be flexible.

Another approach is to offer the company a choice of alternatives. If you have no particular preference, allow the company to decide among them. This demonstrates your willingness to be flexible and calls for a corresponding gesture on the part of the company. It serves the added purpose of bringing the company negotiator into the decision-making process. For instance, you might suggest that you ought to get either a signing bonus or a guarantee of a portion of your first-year bonus. Some companies will not give a signing bonus but will be open to the idea of a guaranteed bonus, whereas others would rather provide a signing bonus and maintain a uniform bonus program without any guarantees. Letting the company choose from among the acceptable options will allow you to achieve your objectives and at the same time enable the company to feel that it has gotten something as well.

I began this book by emphasizing the importance of preparation. Part of that preparation includes determining your negotiating objectives. Being able to make trade-offs requires that you know what your goals are. Be careful, however, to remain flexible. Often when you put a substantial amount of time and energy into preparation, you become blind to opportunities that arise during the course of the negotiations. The problem with a plan, particularly a well-thought-out-plan, is that you tend to stick with it even when things don't turn out exactly as you anticipated. In employment negotiations, as in most types of negotiations, you need to respond to opportunities as they arise.

Young lawyers spend a lot of time preparing. They are hardworking by nature and always want to look as if they know what they are doing. So when they prepare for a deposition, they carefully plan what they are going to ask and meticulously write out all the questions. The only problem with that approach is that they cannot always anticipate what answers they will receive. What sometimes happens is that they continue to ask the prepared questions, failing to follow up on the answers that are given.

Let me give you an example of one such deposition:

> YOUNG LAWYER: What did you do on Christmas Eve, the date of the Seven-Eleven robbery?
>
> WITNESS: I was home wrapping packages all evening.
>
> YOUNG LAWYER: All evening?

WITNESS: All evening.

YOUNG LAWYER: Did you see anyone else that night?

WITNESS: Only my mother, who was home with me all night, and my friend Jay, who works at the Seven-Eleven.

YOUNG LAWYER: Your mother would do anything to keep you out of jail, wouldn't she?

WITNESS: Yes.

YOUNG LAWYER: Even lie for you?

WITNESS: I guess.

The young lawyer is so focused on undermining the credibility of the alibi that she fails to hear, let alone follow up on, how the witness happened to see his friend that evening. So it is, at times, with negotiations. We become so focused on our plan that we miss obvious opportunities.

Before you react to an unanticipated proposal, ask yourself what you could achieve by agreeing to it. Compare the possible financial rewards of that proposal with what you could expect if the company agreed to what you were considering. You need to remain flexible. Negotiating is a dynamic process. Opportunities will arise during the course of the negotiations. All you need to do is recognize them and take advantage of the ones that are presented. As long as you keep your overall objectives firmly in mind, you will be able seize those opportunities as they appear.

Flexibility coupled with a little creativity allowed a friend of mine to take a job that really wanted even though the initial offer was less than she was willing accept. Sally was being considered for a job as director of training at a midsize company. The last person to hold the position had not done a particularly good job and had been encouraged by his boss to leave. The company was able to manage reasonably well for several months without filling the position. Although the president and the vice president of human resources understood the value of having a strong person in that position, others in top management, including the chairman, did not see why the human resources vice president couldn't handle training in addition to her other duties.

The interviewing process took several months. Sally met several times with most of the key members of the management team, including the president and the vice president of human resources. They obviously liked her. She was very interested in the job. Finally she got a call to come in and meet with the two of them. She assumed she would be getting an offer and painstakingly prepared for the meeting. Unfortunately, the negotiations did not proceed as she anticipated.

The president told her that she was the top candidate for the position. However, they had originally been looking for someone not quite as experienced. They had a number of good candidates who were earning substantially less than she was. In light of what the former director of training had been earning, the most they could pay her was $60,000. They told her the company was considering instituting a bonus program but did not currently have one in place. They talked about the potential to grow in the position and to increase her salary once she proved her value to the company. Although she was earning only $55,000 in her current position, she expected to receive a $10,000 performance bonus at the end of the year.

Unlike their previous meetings, this one was very awkward. Sally expressed her interest in the job, but indicated that she was disappointed in the salary being offered. The company's president told her that under the circumstances there wasn't anything more he could do with the salary, but if she had any ideas about other ways to make the offer more attractive he would be glad to entertain them. At that moment she really didn't have any ideas so she decided not to say anything. (See Strategy 23—Silence Is Golden: When to Let the Other Side Talk.) Sally thanked the president and the human resources vice president and said she'd get back to them.

It was clear that Sally really wanted the job. She also believed that there was the possibility of advancement and more money down the road. However, she was not willing to accept less money than she was currently earning. The company's president seemed to be open to improving the offer, but felt constrained by the way the position was viewed by the organization. Sally couldn't easily get the company to increase the salary offer. She needed to be flexible and creative. She had several options. She could try to get the company to give her a car allowance, although that would be unusual for someone at her level. She could seek a salary review in six months, after she had the opportunity to demonstrate what she could do for the company. Alternatively, she could ask for a signing bonus.

Sally decided to ask for a signing bonus to compensate for the bonus she would be losing at her current company. The bonus would not affect the company's salary structure. The company's president seemed to be open to improving the offer, if it did not cause him problems with the other managers or with the chairman. In addition, she asked to be reviewed after six months, by which time she would have shown her value to the company. As it turned out, the president agreed to the signing bonus and to a six-month performance review. The last I heard Sally was enjoying her job and doing well.

Most aspects of any employment agreement are economic. Whether you get paid in the form of a bonus or stock options doesn't matter, provided you have correctly calculated what each will be worth in the end. The negotiating process involves determining available alternatives. Once you know what your options are, you can determine their value as well as your comfort level with the risks involved with each. After you have done so, trade-offs are possible. That is what negotiating is all about.

Summary of Negotiating Points

- Listen.
- Be flexible.
- Be creative.
- Determine your options.
- Evaluate the economic value of the various alternatives.
- Determine your comfort level with each option.
- Be prepared to make trade-offs.

11

Patience, Persistence, and Timing: Outmaneuvering or Outlasting Your Opponent

Nothing in the world can take the place of persistence. Talent will not; nothing is more common than unsuccessful men with talent. Genius will not; unrewarded genius is almost a proverb. Education will not; the world is full of educated failures. Persistence and determination alone are omnipotent.
CALVIN COOLIDGE

Not long ago I represented the senior vice president for sales and market-ing at a large professional services company. He was being recruited for a similar position at a new media company. Because of the new employer's compensation system, typical for that industry, the offer provided for a lower base salary but a higher potential bonus than the executive was receiving in his current position. As a total package, this arrangement was acceptable to my client. However, because the company was in a turn-around situation, severance was a very real issue. My client was justifiably concerned about the proposed terms of his severance arrangement. The company had offered a severance package of one year's base salary and continuation of benefits for one year after termination.

My client discussed his concerns with his prospective boss, the company's president. The president was sympathetic, but deferred to the company's attorney on the issue. When I discussed severance with the attorney, I proposed that my client's targeted bonus be included as part of the severance calculation. The attorney was adamant that the employer could not agree to that proposal. She informed me that no other executives in the company had a severance arrangement which took their bonus into account for the purpose of calculating the amount of severance.

The president was pressing my client to tell his current employer that he was resigning so the company could make a public announcement that he was joining the team. My client was thinking about acquiescing just to be able to reach an agreement quickly. He wanted to try to accommodate the company. However, I persuaded him to call the recruiter who was handling the search and express his reservations about the severance issue. I then called the company's attorney again. I suggested that if the company could not include my client's bonus in determining the sever-ance amount, it should at least provide a severance equal to his current base salary. After all, I argued, it was only fair to do so, because he was taking a cut in base salary to accommodate the company's salary struc-ture. She reacted negatively to the idea but agreed to present my proposal to the president. It was a fair solution to the problem. Even though the lawyer did not like it, my client's situation was unique enough that it did not set a generally applicable precedent. It certainly would not cause the problems that might have resulted if my client were the only executive to have a bonus included in determining the amount of severance. Ultimately the company's president agreed to the proposal, although I am sure over the objections of his attorney. Even though the whole nego-tiating process took only one week, by being patient and persistent we were able to greatly increase the amount of my client's severance.

Two of the most important skills a negotiator can possess are the abil-ity to wait and the ability to say no. In employment negotiations, the ability to say no without angering an adversary is invaluable. If you have ever been in an argument with a determined three year old, you understand the power of persistence. Children simply wear you down until eventually you give in. The same principle applies in employment negotiations, although you need to say no with a great deal more finesse than your average three-year-old uses.

Remember, it is not how quickly you reach an agreement that matters. It's what you end up with that counts. Patience and persistence are often the keys to success. Patience is doubly virtuous during employment negotiations, because time normally works to the employee's advantage. By the time you begin discussing the terms of employment, the company has already made a significant investment in determining whom to hire. With that decision made, the company will be anxious to conclude the deal and move on to other things.

When I say that time generally works in your favor, I am talking about days or at most a few weeks. Sometimes the negotiations will consist of only one or two discussions; at other times they may take weeks. Understanding that we are not talking about extended periods of time, the longer the negotiations last, up to a point, the greater the stake the employer has in ensuring that a successful conclusion is reached. (See Strategy 8—Creating a Stake in the Outcome.)

If something is important to you, refuse to concede the issue. Even as you emphasize areas of agreement, continue to say no to those aspects of the offer which are unacceptable. Be polite. But if the issue is important, keep saying no. State the reasons for your position. Explore alternative ways of satisfying your needs. Do not give in just to conclude the deal.

Sometimes you can best achieve your objectives a little at a time. There is a saying: If you want to get a salami from someone who does not want to give it up, do not ask for the whole thing. Try to get it a slice at a time: one slice now, another later until you have the whole salami. That technique applies in employment negotiations as well.

If you are not making progress, change the subject; come back to the difficult issues later. If you still can't resolve the problem, move on to something else. Return to critical issues as often as necessary. At the same time, listen to the company's objections. Consider those concerns and keep suggesting different options that will not only satisfy your needs but which might also be more acceptable to the company. If you continue to raise the issue periodically, the company will recognize that it is important to you. As the negotiations draw to a conclusion, the company may eventually give in on the issue just to complete the deal. (See Strategy 24—How to Win by Conceding.) If the company cannot agree to what you want because of organizational concerns, it will generally make that clear and you will then have to decide whether to turn down the offer.

Patience will increase your bargaining leverage even more if the company is working under a deadline. In one deal I negotiated for a retail executive, the discussions seemed to go on interminably through no fault of either party. Initially it took days for the company's attorney to get back to me with responses. At some point that changed. He started to return my calls the same day. I knew that the company was putting pressure on him to get the deal done. The attorney had developed a stake in the outcome. The negotiations began to move more quickly. Suddenly the company conceded on some of the key points that remained open.

In addition to patience and persistence, timing is crucial. "When" you say something during negotiations can be as important as "what" you say. Focus on the easy issues first. Ask for something you want after you have made a concession. Don't make all your concessions at once. Consider timing as a key part of your strategy when you are preparing for the negotiations.

Timing the start of compensation discussions, for instance, can have a major impact on how successful you are. It is universally agreed that the best time to begin discussing compensation is after you have been offered the position. At that point, the employer has decided that you are the best candidate for the job. The company wants to hire you and to close the deal quickly. It is then that you are in the best position to negotiate.

Linda Seale, a senior human resources executive and executive coach in New York City, told a story about one of her clients that illustrates the importance of timing. When Sally was first interviewed for a top executive position, the chief executive officer asked, almost immediately, "What are you currently earning?" and "What are you looking for?" Adeptly she responded, "I know salary is important, but to me the challenge and the mandate of the position are more important. I'm happy to discuss compensation but would rather focus on your needs and how I might be able to add value to your company before we discuss money. Can we get back to that at the end of the interview?"

For the next two hours the discussion focused on the job and the goals that needed to be accomplished. Sally offered insights and ideas on how she might accomplish those objectives. She sold her accomplishments. The chemistry was excellent between them. Near the end of the interview her future boss returned to the issue of compensation. Although the recruiter had indicated that he thought the company probably would not pay more than $100,000 for the position, Sally told him that her total compensation was in excess of $100,000 and she was looking for a position in the $125,000 range. After he got to know her and understood what she could do for the company, salary was not even an issue. The chief executive officer asked her if she would be able to meet with some of the other key executives the following week. She was offered the job at a salary that more than met her expectations.

The vice chairman of a Fortune 500 company used timing to great advantage in negotiating an employment agreement. On the day the company announced that it was filing for bankruptcy, he informed the board of directors that he would be leaving to become vice chairman of a competitor. Because of his critical role to the company at that time, he was able to negotiate an agreement which virtually guaranteed that he would become the next chief executive officer. He was also able to negotiate a substantial salary increase. When the chief executive left the company a few months later, the vice chairman was elevated to that position. Even though he probably would have become chief executive officer anyway, his deft use of timing ensured that result.

Patience, persistence, and timing will help you achieve your objectives. You cannot achieve those goals, however, unless you know what they are. By the time you begin to negotiate, you need to have clearly defined your goals and priorities. (See Getting Ready to Negotiate.) Stay focused on your goals. Periodically review the list of priorities you made when you were preparing to negotiate.

Some aspects of a job are negotiable; others are not. The latter are either acceptable to you or they aren't, but they can't be changed. For those things you can obtain through negotiations, you need to determine which are so important that the company's refusal to include them as part of the deal will lead you to decline the offer. For those things that cannot be changed, it is even more important to identify which ones will cause you to turn down the offer. (See Strategy 25—Walking Away.) However, if you are patient and persistent yet open to different ways of satisfying your objectives, you will generally be able to reach an agreement that satisfies everyone's needs.

Summary of Negotiating Points

- Know what your objectives are and your bottom line.
- Consider timing when you are preparing to negotiate.
- Start with the easy issues.
- Be persistent.
- Be prepared to say no if necessary.
- Always say no nicely.
- When you reach an impasse on a key issue, change the subject and return to the issue later.
- Listen and be flexible.
- Be patient.
- Don't agree just to conclude the negotiations quickly.

12

Taking Stock in Your Situation: When and How to Ask for Equity

Because that's where the money is.
WILLIE SUTTON (WHEN ASKED WHY HE
ROBBED BANKS)

In the movie *The Graduate* a guest says to Dustin Hoffman, who plays a recent college graduate: "I have one word for you—plastics." What plastics was in the 1960s, paper is in the 1990s. I'm referring to securities. The key element in an executive's compensation package today is some form of equity, generally stock options.

It is not unusual today for a chief executive officer to receive an annual salary, including bonus, of more than 1 million dollars. The median compensation in 1995 for the chief executive officers surveyed by *Forbes* magazine was $609,000 in base salary and $440,000 in bonus. During this same period, these chief executive officers also realized $695 million in profit from exercising stock options, or almost on average $2.5 million each. The highest-paid chief executive officers in 1995, as in previous years, all received the largest portion of their compensation from exercising stock options or from some other type of equity arrangement. Lawrence Coss of Greentree Financial, the best-paid chief executive officer in 1995, earned a paltry $440,000 in base salary, with the bulk of his $65 million compensation package coming in the form of Greentree stock. Theodore Waitt of Gateway 2000, number two in the survey, received most of his compensation as a result of a $61 million gain from the exercise of stock options. In 1995, Michael Eisner, chief executive officer of Disney, owned $182 million in Disney stock and had stock options worth another $238 million. Moreover, he realized $232 million in compensation during the prior five years, mostly as a result of the miracle of stock options. Obviously there is nothing Mickey Mouse about that.

Stock Options

When I talk about stock options to my business school classes, I refer to them as the best thing that can ever happen to an employee. Bob Corno, a financial adviser at The Mason Companies in Reston, Virginia, once described them to me as "an investment you make with perfect hindsight, offering an infinite return and requiring no investment of money until after the profit is ensured." A stock option grant gives the employee the right to purchase a certain number of shares of the company's stock at a fixed price, usually the market price on the day of the grant. If the price of the company's stock goes up, the employee gets the value of that appreciation. There is no cost to the employee when the options are granted. The employee has no risk. If the price of the underlying stock goes up, the employee stands to make a lot of money. If it goes down, the employee does not lose any money. Moreover, the employee generally does not have to pay any taxes on options, unless the stock goes up in value and the right to purchase the company's stock is exercised. For certain types of options, known as incentive stock options (ISOs), no tax is due until the stock obtained by exercising the options is actually sold. Even then, the employee's profit may be taxable at the lower capital gains rate. It would be hard to design an arrangement that is more favorable for an employee.

Stock Appreciation Rights

Compensation specialists nonetheless continue to come up with new and better ways to use equity to reward key employees. Another type of equity benefit that can be provided to employees is stock appreciation rights (SARs). SARs provide an employee with the right to receive the increase in value of the employer's stock between the date the SARs are granted and the date they are exercised. SARs are similar to stock options except that employees don't have to actually pay any money to exercise them. SARs are often granted along with stock options. Sometimes SARs can be exercised only in lieu of the stock options (tandem SARs), giving employees the choice of which to exercise. Employers can also grant SARs that are exercisable together with stock options (nontandem SARs). In this case, employees can use the proceeds from the exercise of nontandem SARs to pay the exercise price for the related stock options and the required withholding taxes as well.

Restricted Stock

Employers may also grant restricted stock to key employees. This type of stock is given outright if employees meet certain conditions. For example, employees may be conditionally granted restricted stock which they will earn if they remain with the company for a specified period of time. Awards of restricted stock are often conditioned on meeting certain performance goals. Like stock options, restricted stock is issued at no cost. But unlike stock options, which provide the right to purchase the stock at a fixed price, shares of restricted stock are simply given to the employee once the conditions are met. The employee gets the full value of the restricted stock, not just the appreciation following the date of the grant.

Phantom Stock

Another form of equity which can be used to reward employees is phantom stock. Phantom stock can be converted into an equal number of shares of the company's stock or into their cash value at a specified future date. Phantom stock usually can be converted only after the employee has remained with the company for a certain number of years. An award of phantom stock may also be conditioned on meeting certain performance goals. Phantom stock entitles the employee not only to the value of the stock but also to the dividends paid on the actual shares. Normally the dividends are paid at the same time the phantom stock is converted. As with restricted stock, the executive gets the full value of the shares, and the value of the phantom stock is not taxed until the employee has the right to convert it.

Stock Purchase Requirements

A number of companies now require high-level executives to purchase a certain amount of the company's stock with their own money. The rationale for requiring stock ownership is to better align the executive's interests with those of the stockholders. The theory is that when executives have their own money at risk, they will focus on increasing shareholder value. If your employment agreement includes a requirement of this type, the employer will normally offer you a loan to facilitate the purchase as part of your compensation package. At the very least, you ought to seek an interest-free loan to finance the stock purchase. It is better, however, if you can get a signing bonus to cover the cost of the stock. As this concept catches on, you can expect it to filter down to lower-level employees, probably in the form of providing incentives for them to purchase and hold company stock. Depending on the nature of the program, you may need to consider required stock purchases in developing your negotiating strategy.

The Equity Package

There are other ways for companies to provide equity to their employees. No doubt creative lawyers and accountants will devise new methods in the future. Providing equity to key employees benefits the company as well as the employees. It encourages them to remain with the company and to find ways to increase the value of the company's stock. For an employee, getting stock from a new employer, in whatever form, will ordinarily be the quickest route to financial well-being.

Much of my bargaining effort on behalf of executives has been spent negotiating over the amount of equity they will receive and under what conditions they will get to keep it. In many instances, executives earning substantial salaries and bonuses are leaving large companies because they are eager to receive a greater portion of their compensation in the form of stock or options. A major element of negotiating these deals is to determine how much stock, and in what form, an executive should be provided in light of what he or she is giving up.

I recall one agreement I negotiated on behalf of an executive who had been receiving large annual cash bonuses from his employer. His prospective employer, a small high-tech company, was in no position to provide bonuses of that magnitude. What it could provide was a substantial amount of equity. So that was what we sought.

The first thing we did was make sure my client received his most recent bonus before leaving his current employer. (See Strategy 6—Timing Your Departure.) Next we attempted to value the stock of his prospective employer. We looked at the company's earnings history and projected an annual growth rate of about 5 percent. On the basis of that projection, we sought a grant of a certain amount of restricted stock which, in accordance with the company's practice, would vest over a four-year period. Additional restricted stock would be granted a year later, when my client was to be promoted. We also sought, and received, the company's agreement to provide grants of a fixed number of stock options each year during the term of the agreement. The amount of these grants would increase if certain performance targets were reached.

The primary focus of the bargaining was to maximize the amount of equity my client received. Whenever the employer balked at a request, we returned to how much my client was giving up in cash bonuses by leaving his current employer. We emphasized that any increase in the value of the company's stock would be, at least in part, a result of my client's efforts. If he did not do a good job and the company did not prosper, he would not reap any benefit. Moreover, because he was accepting equity in lieu of a cash bonus, regardless of how well he performed, a major part of his compensation would now be subject to the vagaries of the stock market. In the end, we were able to get sufficient stock so that within four years, if our projections were met or exceeded, my client would be significantly better off with the new company's stock than he would have been with the bonuses from his prior employer. An added benefit of structuring a compensation package to include a greater proportion of equity is the tax advantage that stock and stock options provide.

The above example is a typical equity package that a key executive can obtain from a company that either does not want to or is not in a position to match the employee's current cash compensation. Under these circumstances, a highly sought-after key executive will almost always be able to obtain an equity stake in the company. How large an equity position you receive will depend on how much the company wants to recruit you and how well you negotiate. A fairly common tactic is to constantly remind the company of how much you are giving up by accepting the job, in order to persuade the employer to increase the amount of equity in the deal.

Unfortunately, unless you are a high-level executive, there is no surefire method to get a prospective employer to give you stock and/or options when you change jobs. For most of us, getting an equity stake in a company depends more on the company we join than on our negotiating prowess. Most large publicly traded companies have stock option plans, but participation tends to be limited to executives above a certain level. Therefore your eligibility to participate in the program will depend on your position within the organization. (See Strategy 4—Negotiate the Position, Not the Salary.) Most employees have access only to stock purchase plans. These plans allow them to purchase a certain amount of company stock at a discount each year. Although eligibility to participate in a stock purchase plan is an excellent benefit, you are unlikely to be lunching with Michael Eisner as a result of your participation.

When can an employee who is not a senior level executive expect to negotiate an employment deal that includes stock or stock options? When the employee chooses the right company. Large publicly traded companies don't offer stock options to most of their employees. Family-owned companies are even less likely to offer stock to employees who are not family members. However, many start-up companies, particularly high-tech companies, will offer stock options to employees with critical skills. Typically these companies can't afford to pay top dollar to hire the employees they want. They are often strapped for cash. In order to attract the talent they need, start-up companies regularly offer stock options to new hires. Ask the secretaries or programmers who started with Microsoft 20 years ago whether taking a lower salary in return for stock options was a good decision. Today many of them are millionaires.

If you choose the right company, you may be able to negotiate a compensation package that includes stock or stock options. If so, you can use the negotiating strategies described in this book to increase the amount of stock that you are offered. A small start-up company is likely to be flexible in what it is willing to do to make up for your having to accept a lower salary. That route may turn out to be a good one for you financially, provided you can afford to take a cut in salary. The key is to select a company that will grow and be able to go public within a reasonable time. If the company you join is successful, those stock options may prove to be very valuable.

Keep in mind, however, that although equity offers the potential for large financial rewards, there is no guarantee of riches. Sometimes companies don't do well and your options expire worthless. As many of us have learned from personal experience, even good companies can end up in bankruptcy. Notwithstanding the fact that you have negotiated brilliantly and have received a substantial equity stake, the value of that stock will depend on how well the company does. Even if the company prospers, its stock may be affected by gyrations in the stock market unrelated to how well the business is being run. Timing and luck will also generally play a role in the value of your stock. Therefore, when you are considering taking equity instead of salary or bonuses, you need to consider not only what you are able to get the company to agree to but also your current financial needs and your tolerance for risk.

Summary of Negotiating Points

- Determine how much of your compensation you feel comfortable taking in the form of equity.

- If equity is important to you, look for companies that offer stock to employees at your level.

- Carefully evaluate the financial prospects of the company.

- Determine the types of equity plans available to employees at various levels.

- Negotiate participation in the best plan for which you could be eligible (or negotiate a higher-level position).

- Consider the possibility of trading salary for equity.

- Don't become enamored with the idea of getting stock and give up too much in order to get it. If you are paid enough money, you can always buy the stock.

- Remember that equity offers not only rewards but risks as well.

13

Using Another Offer Even When You Don't Have One

*Of the things you have select the best; and
then reflect how eagerly they would have been
sought if you did not have them.*
MARCUS AURELIUS

If you have been to an auction, you know that the best thing that can ever happen to a seller is to have two bidders become emotionally involved in the bidding. The bidders soon care more about winning than they do about the prize. Inevitably the winner pays more for the item being auctioned than it is worth. If you can replicate this situation in the employment context, you are certain to maximize your compensation.

Such a strategy must be pursued very carefully, especially if you are using it with your current employer. Although companies value employees whose talents are sought after by others, they also value loyalty. If your employer finds out that you are negotiating with another company, it may promptly show you the door. Just as often, your employer will try to convince you to stay by outbidding the other company. Ordinarily, along with the counterbid the company will begin the search for a potential replacement. After all, if you've threatened to leave once for more money, sooner or later you can be expected to do so again.

Using Another Offer with Your Current Employer

What good is getting another offer if using it to improve your current compensation will cause your employer to consider you disloyal? If you understand how to use it, you are always in a better position for having received another offer of employment. In the first place, you may decide to accept the offer. Moreover, at the very least, it tells you something about your market value. If your employer has consistently paid you less than you could command elsewhere, you may want to consider a move even if this is not the one. Finally, if you use the offer properly, you can improve your current situation without being considered disloyal. In fact, it is possible to demonstrate your loyalty and get your present employer to give you a raise at the same time.

Consider the following situation. Tom had just been offered a position as the chief operating officer at a consumer products company. He was currently the chief operating officer of one of its competitors. Tom liked the company he was working for and was in line to become its chief executive officer, but the company would not commit to giving him the job when it became available. The offer he received from the competitor was for a lot more money than he was then making. More important, it gave him an opportunity to become chief executive officer within a few years.

At this point I came into the negotiations. We quickly reached agreement with the competitor on salary and bonus. After some hard bargaining, we were also able to agree on a very generous package of restricted stock and stock options. Details of the move were worked out and I thought we would soon have a deal. Then we started discussing protections in the event things didn't work out—severance, reasons for discharge, rights in the event of a takeover, and most important to my client, a commitment and timetable for him to become chief executive officer. Despite a great deal of effort, we were unable to get the company to provide sufficient guarantees to make it worthwhile for my client to leave his current position. As sometimes happens when a company bargains too long and too hard over the wrong issues, my client soured on the deal. Tom thanked me for my help and told me that even if we were able to work out adequate protections, he was no longer interested. He was prepared to stay in his current job and wait for his shot at being made chief executive officer. If that didn't happen, perhaps a better offer would come along in the interim.

I suggested another option. He could tell his current employer about the offer and use it as leverage. He took that advice. Tom told his boss, the current chief executive officer, that he had received an offer from a competitor to be chief operating officer, and he spelled out the terms of the deal we had negotiated. He also told his boss, who intended to retire some time during the next few years, that he was not going to accept the offer. Tom informed him that the only reason he had even considered the offer was that the board of directors had declined to make any commitments about his future with the company. He then asked his boss if he would be willing to try to get the board of directors to do something about that.

Tom did two things that enabled him to make use of a competing offer without jeopardizing his current position. First, he informed his boss that he was not going to accept the offer, thereby avoiding the perception that the company was being presented with an ultimatum. Second, he explained why he was tempted by the offer and enlisted his boss's help in trying to resolve his concerns. By so doing, he reaffirmed his loyalty to the company and made his boss an ally in helping him get the commitment he wanted. He also avoided creating an adversarial situation which would require his current employer to respond to a competing bid for his services. By telling his boss about the offer, Tom supplied the ammunition that was needed to get the board of directors to take action. Although the directors would not give him any guarantees about being promoted to chief executive officer, they did indicate that he was their number-one candidate at the moment. They also agreed, as part of an extension of his employment contract, to match the offer he had received. In addition, they agreed that if he was not made chief executive officer within a specified amount of time, he could leave with a generous severance package. Within two years Tom was promoted to chief executive officer.

Not everyone is a potential chief executive officer. Nor can we all expect to regularly get unsolicited offers from prospective employers. However, those of us who are being paid less than the current market rate for what we do can use that knowledge to attempt to remedy the situation. The first step is to find out what others are getting paid in comparable jobs. There are various ways to get that information. Check the want ads. Join a networking group such as Exec-U-Net, based in Weston, Connecticut, whose members share information about job openings. Look at market surveys. Make use of the resources available on the Internet. (See Getting Ready to Negotiate.) Generally keep your ear to the ground. If you hear about a job that interests you, contact the company. If you decide the job is not right for you, you may want to casually let your employer know that another company expressed interest in hiring you for a better-paying job, even though you were not interested.

A word of caution is necessary here. Even if you have a firm offer in hand, don't make your employer feel that you are presenting an ultimatum. If you do, you had better be prepared to accept the offer, because there is a good chance that your employer will immediately escort you out. Even if you aren't let go, you are likely never to be completely trusted again. Your employer will always be wondering when you are going to level another ultimatum.

When Two Potential Employers Are Interested in You

Using another offer with your present employer is one thing. Using a second offer with an employer that is trying to recruit you is a wholly different matter. This is the best situation you can ever find yourself in. Here there is no issue of loyalty. You are free to create a bidding war if you can. Still, you need to proceed carefully. An employer that is seeking to recruit you may resent it if you appear to be playing one company against the other. No one likes to feel they are being manipulated. You need to avoid making people you are negotiating with feel that way.

If two companies are trying to hire you, all things being equal you will likely choose the highest bidder. In real life, unfortunately, all things are rarely ever equal. You are almost always going to prefer one company or one boss over another. One company will offer more opportunity for growth or more stability. The key, then, is to use the interest of the other company to improve the offer from the company you prefer.

How do you accomplish that? I recommend that you refer to the fifth commandment of employment negotiations: "Never lie, but use the truth to your advantage." Once you have an offer from each, try to get the less favored company to improve its offer. Since this company is not your first choice, you will be able to push hard to get the offer improved. In the end, it won't really matter whether you reach an agreement. After all, your objective is to use the discussions to improve your bargaining position with the other company. Once you have gotten as much as you can, you can go to your prospective boss at the preferred company and honestly say: "I have this very generous offer from another company, but the truth is I'd much rather work for you. However, I just can't ignore the gap between what it is offering and what you are offering. If you could just get the company to put together a package that is in the same ballpark, I would start tomorrow."

Sometimes one offer will be so much better than the other that there is no possibility that the lower bidder will be able to match the better offer. If the lower bidder is the company you would prefer to work for and you are willing to accept a lesser offer, you can relatively easily use the higher offer to get the other company to improve its proposal. If, on the other hand, the offer from the preferred company is already much better than the competing offer, you can still use the fact that you have another offer to your advantage. Obviously, you don't want to discuss the terms of the competing offer. Let the preferred company know that you would very much like to work there. Mention the areas of concern you have and stress that, if you can work them out to everyone's satisfaction, you will accept the job. Remind the employer that, even though you would prefer to work there, you are still talking to the other company.

Similarly, even if you don't actually have another offer, you can improve your bargaining position just by talking to another employer at the same time as you are negotiating an offer. In the first place, the fact that you have other possibilities will provide you with the confidence needed to insist on getting what you are worth. It will also give you the courage to walk away if you don't. Moreover, the fact that someone else may enter into the bidding will pressure the preferred company to complete the negotiations quickly and to give you its best offer. This tactic will work even if you initiate the discussions with the other company and even if there is no actual job currently available. You don't have to inform your prospective employer of the exact nature of your discussions—only that you are having such discussions with another employer.

Some experts would suggest that you "accidentally" let the preferred company find out that you are talking to someone else. You might casually let people there see something from the other company, such as a business card or an annual report. Alternatively, when you are visiting with one prospective employer, you might ask a secretary there to place a call to the other company for you. The problem with this approach is that you can never be sure if the appropriate people have actually found out what you want them to know. I prefer the more direct and honest approach. Simply tell people that, although you would really like to work for their company, you are also talking to a competitor and you didn't want them to find that out from someone else. Your candor will not only improve your bargaining position but will enhance your credibility as well.

In short, you will get a better deal any time someone with whom you are negotiating knows that you have other options. Therefore, whenever possible, you should create those options for yourself or at least create the illusion that they exist. Once you have done that, be sure to let the appropriate people know about it.

Summary of Negotiating Points

- Having another offer will almost always improve your bargaining position.
- Be careful how you use other offers.
- Talking to a competitor may be considered an act of disloyalty by your current employer.
- Let your current employer know about a competing offer by announcing that you are not going to accept it.
- Inform your employer of the reasons you were willing to consider the offer and ask if the company can address your concerns.
- Don't make an employer feel that you are presenting an ultimatum.
- Create other potential offers for yourself by talking to companies that might be interested in you.
- If you have two offers, before using the offer from your second choice as leverage, try to get the company to improve it.
- Even if you don't actually have another offer, it is helpful (at an appropriate time) to let your first choice know you are talking to another company.

14
Not Negotiating as a Strategy

It is noble to spare the vanquished.

STATIUS

The toughest time to negotiate is when you have little or no bargaining power and the other side knows it. Under those circumstances the best thing to do is to use the techniques discussed in this book to give the illusion that your bargaining position is better than it actually is. (See Strategy 13—Using Another Offer Even When You Don't Have One.) There will be times, however, when you are not in a position to do even that. One of those times is when you are willing to accept the particular job without regard to the financial arrangements, because you are reluctant to take any risk that might cause the deal to fall through. Generally it is not a good idea to allow yourself psychologically to be in that position, since the company's negotiator will recognize it and will use it to your disadvantage.

Unless you are willing to take some risk, you will never be able to negotiate effectively. You will usually end up just accepting whatever the company initially offers. Unfortunately, the company's first offer is not ordinarily its best offer. Nonetheless, there may be any number of reasons why you may not want to negotiate. You may be out of work. (See When You're Unemployed: How to Gain Bargaining Leverage Even If You Think You Have None.) You may view this job as a once-in-a-lifetime opportunity or you may simply not want to take any chances with the offer. In such cases, there is little you can do to improve the offer other than to employ a strategy based on not negotiating. This strategy is designed to avoid jeopardizing the offer. If you are willing to take some risk, however, there may be other strategies that are more effective.

One time when a strategy of not negotiating may be appropriate is when you are just starting out in your career. As a recent graduate, you generally will not have any unique skills or experience which qualify you for the position you are seeking. Often you are being selected for the position on the basis of your potential. The company that hires you will have to spend time and money training you. Ordinarily when you apply for a job right out of school you are one of many candidates who could be trained to do the job. Unless you graduated from an especially prestigious university, have an outstanding academic record, possess some unique talent, or are lucky enough to graduate at a time when labor is in short supply, you will have very little bargaining power. Under these circumstances there is very little that you can do to improve your bargaining position. That is when the only viable strategy for most people is not to negotiate.

A friend once asked me if I would talk to his son Sean about a job offer he was considering. Sean was a recent college graduate who had majored in business. He had sought out a position with a real estate developer in Los Angeles because of the company's excellent reputation. He had convinced the company to offer him a job. Sean considered this an excellent opportunity to learn the business. His only concern was about the salary. Since his parents were in New Jersey, he would not be able to make ends meet by living at home. He told me he didn't want his parents to continue to support him. He was worried about being able to get by in Los Angeles on the salary being offered. Although Sean had other job possibilities, none offered the same chance to gain this type of experience. It was an opportunity to do something that he really wanted to do. It was very clear that, for him, salary was not the most important issue.

In light of all these factors, it seemed obvious to me that "not negotiating" was the most appropriate approach for Sean to use. In fact, under the circumstances it may have been the only plausible strategy for him to employ in order to try to improve the offer. Therefore we discussed how he could "negotiate" a better deal by not negotiating.

He called the person who offered him the job and for whom he would be working. The conversation went something like this:

STUDENT: I'm very excited about the position and am going to accept it. I'm really looking forward to working with you at Big California Realty Developer. Although I have other job offers which pay more, this is the only place I want to work. Would the company, however, consider increasing the starting salary? I think it is low and I know I will have a tough time being able to live on that salary in Los Angeles. I want you to understand that if you can't do anything about the salary I still want the job. However, I would appreciate anything you could do for me.

FUTURE BOSS: I'll see what I can do.

In the end Sean was given a relocation bonus to help him make the move and the promise of a raise in six months if he did a good job.

Sean got what he wanted by not negotiating. After all, he really was not in much of a position to negotiate. He had no experience; there were probably hundreds of other students who would have jumped at the opportunity to take this job. He might have told the company that he had other job offers at higher salaries and would accept one unless the employer came up with more money. The company would probably have responded by telling him to go ahead. Instead, Sean accepted the job unconditionally and asked for help so he could afford to move to Los Angeles.

I cannot emphasize enough that the key to being successful in negotiating employment terms is to understand the role that fairness plays in the process. Fairness is paramount. It is the guiding principle that determines what an employer is willing to offer. If you can convince the employer that what you are seeking is fair, you have a good chance of getting it. In order to do that, you need to have facts to support your request. If an offer is below the market rate for the position, you need to be able to demonstrate that the salary being offered is too low. If you are going to rely on are your personal situation to support a particular request, you should describe your needs in a way that will evoke sympathetic understanding.

Always bear in mind that employers want to make the people they are trying to recruit happy. At this stage, the company is still in the courtship phase of its relationship with you. It is very open to reasonable requests. A strategy of not negotiating recognizes, and takes advantage of, these basic principles. It also takes a realistic view of the relative bargaining positions of the parties. This approach employs the classic negotiating technique of taking a weakness and turning it into a strength. You do that by seeking out the help of the company's negotiator.

As a child, you were taught a sense of fair play. When you have bested someone, you are suppose to be gracious. When the game is over for all intents and purposes, you don't run up the score. You help those who are weaker and who need assistance. Throw yourself on the mercy of the company's negotiator. Appeal to this sense of fairness.

This tactic works more often than not. Moreover, it is a very low risk strategy. After all, you have nothing to lose. However, you should employ this strategy only when you are willing to accept an offer even if the company refuses to change it. In fact, the strategy begins by your accepting the offer that has been made. Then, and only then, do you begin trying to convince your future employer that fairness calls for a modification in the terms. If you utilize this strategy effectively, the company will resolve your concerns even though it knows that it doesn't have to.

Summary of Negotiating Points

- Understand when not to negotiate.
- Accept the offer.
- Ask for help.
- Appeal to fairness.
- Play on the employer's sympathy.
- Have facts to support your request.

15
Creating Red Herring Issues

Appearances often are deceiving.   AESOP

When herring are smoked and salted, they turn a brownish-red color. The British refer to these smoked fish as "red herring." In addition to being a delicacy, these fish have a distinct smell. In eighteenth-century England, opponents of fox hunting were able to put these fish to good use in furthering their cause. Animal rights activists of their day did whatever they could to prevent the hunts from taking place. One of the ways they disrupted the hunts was to drag a red herring across the hunting trail. The smell of the herring would confuse the hunting dogs and prevent them from picking up the scent of the fox. This practice gave rise to the phrase "red herring" to refer to a distraction from the real issues. In basketball, it is called a fake. In negotiating, a red herring issue is one that you don't really care about but introduce in order to be able to withdraw later in return for some concession.

Creating red herring issues is a common practice used in negotiating collective-bargaining agreements. Union negotiations, which typically involve a large negotiating committee, require a visible display of the process of give-and-take. When the negotiations are over, both sides need to believe that they got the best possible deal. The red herring tactic is less commonly used in negotiating employment agreements and when it is, no one admits to it. In fact, some consider it unethical.

Nonetheless, the need for some give-and-take is just as important in employment negotiations as it is in other types of negotiations.

If you insist on getting everything that you ask for before you will accept an employment offer, you are likely to remain in your current job for a very long time. Even if you do reach an agreement on that basis, it will be probably at the expense of goodwill: Your future employer will feel that you have driven too hard a bargain. Maintaining some bargaining issues that you are willing to compromise on will make it much easier to reach an agreement that is satisfactory to all parties. Using red herring issues for that purpose will enable you not to give up other concerns that are more important to you.

The process sounds easier than it actually is. You need to be very cautious as to how you use red herring issues when negotiating the terms of your employment. In the collective-bargaining process, everyone knows from the start that some of the issues raised are red herrings: in employment negotiations, that is not the case. It is inappropriate to raise issues that you really do not care about with a potential employer. In this context, *red herring issues should be reasonable requests for things that you would like but that you really don't expect your prospective employer to agree to.* These issues will provide you with room to negotiate. It would be nice if you could get the company to agree to these points, but their principal value is that they can be traded away for other items that are more important to you.

Let's assume, for example, that you have received an offer to be director of marketing for a new restaurant venture, Planet Poughkeepsie. You like the company. You like the way the job is set up. The salary and benefits are good, but you haven't been offered any stock options. You believe that the company will soon go public and that stock options will be very valuable. What do you do?

You could simply ask for the options. The company might give them to you. On the other hand, the restaurant might say that it has already offered you a generous salary and will consider giving you options only after you prove yourself. Alternatively, you could not only ask for the options but also note that in your current job you have a company car, another feature lacking in the restaurant's offer. You might also ask if the position could be restructured at the vice president level. You would like the car and a better title, but what you really want are the stock options. You know, because of the impact these changes would have on the organization (other executives at your level are not given cars or the title of vice president), that the easiest of the three requests for the company to grant is the stock options. By asking about the car and the title, you have created red herring issues that you will be able to sacrifice if the company grants you the stock options you really want.

You can also raise red herring issues by refusing to agree to something that you recognize the company wants. Let's assume that you know that every executive in the company signs a noncompete agreement. The basic form of the agreement never varies. Although you would like fewer restrictions on where you can work after you leave Mega Corp., this issue is of much less concern to you than your salary. How can you use your knowledge that every new employee signs the same noncompete agreement to your advantage? Consider the following approach:

YOU: I was speaking to my lawyer about that noncompete agreement you told me I would have to sign.

NEGOTIATOR: And?

YOU: He has some concerns.

NEGOTIATOR: Really it's no big deal. Everyone signs it.

YOU: If it's no big deal, why don't we just make the changes he is suggesting and move on?

NEGOTIATOR: I can't do that.

YOU: Well, I don't know anything about agreements not to compete. But if my lawyer is telling me I should be concerned, I guess I need to be concerned. I'll talk to him. I'm sure that if we can resolve my problems with the bonus criteria, we will be able to work out something on the noncompete.

Your concerns are real, since your lawyer will no doubt have misgivings about any noncompete agreement you are asked to sign. However, what you have done is create a red herring issue over the company's demand that you sign its standard noncompete agreement. You have made one issue conditional upon the other. Your willingness to accept the noncompete agreement will depend on the company offering you a more favorable bonus plan. If the company negotiator has any leeway at all, the bonus criteria will be modified to incorporate any reasonable suggestions you make. Moreover, you have the added benefit of blaming your concerns about the agreement not to compete on your lawyer. Whenever possible, this is a good thing to do. (See Strategy 16— Blaming the Lawyers, Accountants, and Others.)

As previously discussed, the key to negotiating terms of employment is convincing your prospective employer that what you are seeking is fair. Therefore anything you ask for during the course of negotiations should be reasonable and defensible. Similarly, if you are not willing to agree to something, be certain that you can articulate a rationale for your position. Otherwise your credibility will be undermined. By the same token, you cannot expect to get everything you ask for. As a result, the discriminating use of red herring issues can be very effective.

Summary of Negotiating Points

- Negotiating calls for give-and-take.
- Don't expect to get everything you ask for.
- Red herring issues should be reasonable requests for improvements in the offer that you would like but don't necessarily expect to get.
- Raise red herring issues so that you have something to trade at key points during the negotiations.
- You can create red herring issues by refusing to agree to something the employer wants in order to obtain bargaining leverage.
- Be very careful how you use the red herring tactic if you choose to use it at all.

16

Blaming the Lawyers, Accountants, and Others

It's not whether you win or lose but how you place the blame. ANONYMOUS

Before we discuss how to blame your lawyers, let me offer some advice on how to use your lawyers. Lawyers and accountants can serve an important function in employment negotiations. They are advisers. If they are good at what they do, their advice will be very useful. They can anticipate problems and help you avoid them. They can assist you in developing negotiating strategies. They can even help you decide what is really important to you. They are not, however—nor should they be—the ones making the critical decisions. When they do, the negotiations often turn into a contest. The primary focus of the lawyer then becomes winning. Your goal is not to win but rather to get what is important to you.

Decisive executives suddenly become insecure when they are negotiating about their own future. I have seen executives who regularly negotiate deals worth millions of dollars defer completely to the advice of lawyers when it comes to their own employment. Only you know what is important to you. When the negotiations are over, your lawyer will go back to other clients. You, on the other hand, will have to work alongside the people with whom you are negotiating.

Choose knowledgeable lawyers and accountants. Listen to their advice, but make up your own mind. Lawyers and accountants are trained to identify risks and to try to protect against them. Although they can help you develop strategies to achieve your goals, ultimately you have to decide what those goals are. You have to decide how much risk you are comfortable taking. An accountant can value stock options, but only you can decide if you are willing to accept a lower salary in return for a certain number of stock options.

Normally I advise against having your lawyer or accountant directly involved in the negotiations, at least initially. Usually you can achieve better results by directly negotiating as much of the deal as you can yourself, seeking advice as necessary. Lawyers and accountants will generally serve you better in the role of behind-the-scenes advisers.

Unless I am representing very high-level executives, who customarily have lawyers negotiate their employment contracts, I almost never negotiate directly on behalf of a client until after the company's attorney is already involved. Since the person you will negotiate with is likely to be your future boss or a human resources executive responsible for filling the position, that person has a personal stake in seeing that you are hired. As a result, that individual will almost always be more generous than the company's lawyer, who has different objectives. Since having someone else, particularly your lawyer, negotiate on your behalf is likely to result in the company bringing its lawyer into the process, as a rule it is not a good idea to do so. Lawyers will almost always slow up the negotiations and will frequently make them more difficult.

Inevitably the company's attorney has an agenda, which rarely has anything to do with satisfying your needs. It probably has more to do with impressing the client. Also, a lawyer will be very concerned with setting precedents that might cause problems in the future. The company's lawyer will want to give away as little as possible and still get you to accept the job. That is how a lawyer determines the success of the negotiations. Your future boss, on the other hand, is more likely to judge the success of the negotiations by whether the agreement is fair and whether you feel comfortable with it. Unless you are talking about technical legal issues which only lawyers understand, you are almost always better off dealing directly with someone at the company, preferably your future boss. Even when the lawyers are negotiating between themselves, if there are major points of contention it is often better for you to go back to the company negotiator to resolve those issues.

So unless the company's lawyer is already taking an active role in the negotiations, it is best to not bring your attorney into the picture until it serves some tactical purpose. The same advice applies to using an accountant or anyone else to negotiate actively on your behalf.

Gaining Credibility and Expertise

When does it make sense for executives to use someone else to negotiate on their behalf? There are a number of reasons they might want to do so. First, they may simply not be good negotiators. This is unusual for executives, since negotiating is ordinarily an important part of their job. However, sometimes people are successful because of their technical expertise or their ability to inspire and motivate others or for some other reason that has nothing to do with being good negotiators. In that case, it may be best to have someone else handle the negotiations.

Another time to involve your lawyer is when the company already has its attorney actively involved in the negotiations and you need to "even up the sides." Doing so will prevent the company from taking advantage of you by getting you to agree to something, the implications of which you don't fully understand. It will also prevent the company from trying to use the lawyer's "expertise" to intimidate you. When the company's lawyer says to you "That is the way we always do it," you want to have a lawyer involved who can respond that she always does it some other way. Using your own lawyer will enable you to avoid appearing intransigent by refusing to agree to something that the company's lawyer claims is not only reasonable but customary. Moreover, most people feel more secure having their own lawyer present when they are negotiating with a lawyer. Finally, if the negotiations become difficult, having your lawyer along provides you with a means of taking the company's attorney out of the picture. When the time is right, you can simply suggest that the parties sit down without the lawyers and try to work something out.

You may also want to use your lawyer as an "expert," to lend credibility to your position. If the facts support your point of view, having an expert present them can add weight to your position. If, for example, the salary being offered is below what other companies are paying for similar positions, you might have your lawyer or accountant present that information. If the negotiations are not at a level where it would make sense to bring your lawyer or accountant to the table, you can simply invoke that expertise when you present the information (as in "My financial adviser tells me...").

Most often, however, you will inject someone else into the negotiations because you need to raise an issue that might upset your future employer. Using a lawyer enables you to take positions you would not otherwise be able to take. In addition, your attorney only has limited authority and can make use of that fact. This enables your lawyer to seek concessions without being able to make them.

One way to make the most of these dynamics is to have your lawyer deal directly with the company's lawyer on technical or drafting issues while you continue to discuss substantive issues with the company negotiator. For example, about a year ago I represented the senior vice president of human resources of a publishing company who was being recruited for a similar position at another company. As is frequently the case these days, the amount of severance he would receive was an issue. The company had offered him a severance of six months' salary continuation minus any salary earned from other employment during that period. We were seeking one year's severance without regard to any income earned elsewhere. Therefore, not only was the amount of severance an issue but also whether it would be reduced by the amount of money he earned from other employment during the severance period.

The company was a takeover target. Since my client had two children in college, he was especially concerned about job security over the next two years. He wanted a severance package that was sufficient in light of his need to make monthly tuition payments for his children. He discussed those concerns with his future boss. At the same time, I began talks with the company's attorney about a number of other issues. When we discussed severance, I asked for one year to be paid in a lump sum at the time of termination. The company's attorney was not willing to offer more than six months' severance, and insisted that it be paid as salary continuation. She was adamant that the company could not agree to our proposal because every other company executive participated in a severance plan which provided for a maximum of six months severance, which was paid as salary continuation.

After talking to my client, I suggested that he again discuss his concern about the issue with his future boss, the company's president. He told the president that I had suggested that the company give him a signing bonus if the severance package could not be improved. I made the same proposal to the company's attorney. After all, I argued, it was only fair, since my client was giving up a relatively secure job to join a company that could be taken over in the near future. By giving my client a bonus rather than changing the structure of its severance plan, the company would not stir up problems with its other executives. However, in the event my client lost his job because of a takeover, he would have the bonus money available to pay his children's tuition. Ultimately, the company agreed to this arrangement. It addressed my client's concerns and did not create problems with the company's other executives.

I was not intimidated by the lawyer's invoking her expertise to support the claim that the company could not agree to enhance the severance package because of the precedent it would set. I was able to make a strong argument based on fairness. I was also able to propose an alternative solution, which the company could not refuse on the grounds of setting a precedent. I could do the things that my client needed done but that he could not do for himself. He could not argue this point as strongly as I could. It would have been much harder for him to suggest a signing bonus than it was for me. Most important, even though I don't know if he would have walked away from the deal over this issue, he never had to make that decision. Because it was my proposal, if the company's president had reacted badly to it, my client could still have accepted the offer without losing credibility with his future boss.

Tackling the Difficult Issues

Lawyers, accountants, and other intermediaries can do things you cannot do. They can take more aggressive positions than you might feel comfortable taking yourself. They can argue much more forcefully than you could, particularly when they are dealing with the company's lawyers. They can float "trial balloons" to see what kind of reaction they get, making clear that the proposals are their ideas, not yours. If the company reacts negatively to the positions being taken by a professional on your behalf, you are free to disavow them. If someone at the company gets angry over the way your lawyer is negotiating, you can apologize for the lawyer's behavior. In the worst case, if the deal is about to fall apart, you can always blame it all on your lawyer and smooth matters over directly with the company. This is what the CIA calls maintaining "deniability."

Similarly, you may be able to ask for things on behalf of your spouse or your children, even though those things "cost" the company. When you are changing jobs, other people's needs have to be considered. Your spouse or significant other and your children all will have something to say about your changing jobs. Typically family issues come to the forefront when a move is involved. Concerns about housing, schools, and the careers of trailing spouses are common. A *New York Times* poll recently reported that relocation executives expected a substantial increase in the number of requests for help in finding jobs for spouses, help with schools, and assistance in finding care facilities for elderly parents. Any experienced recruiter knows that the wishes of family members will often determine whether someone accepts a job offer. Most company negotiators will be sympathetic to your need to make your family happy or to address the concerns of a working spouse. As a result, companies are generally receptive to reasonable requests related to family needs.

Sometimes these issues, particularly second-career issues, can be dealt with through resources readily available to the company. A few calls from a company executive to contacts at other companies in town can often open doors for job interviews. Relationships with executive recruiters can be called upon. Potential job openings within the company can be considered. Some issues can be solved only by more money. To get your family to leave a house that you have just completely redecorated may require you to purchase an even bigger home in your new community and to have the funds available to redecorate it. In order to do that, you may need to ask for a signing bonus. When you give a reason for seeking the bonus instead of simply asking for one, your request is more likely to be sympathetically received.

Since you will ultimately have to work with the people you are bargaining with, a lawyer, accountant, or other intermediary can be especially valuable in employment negotiations. An intermediary can do those things which are sometimes strategically necessary but which you could only do at the cost of damaging your future career. Rather than not doing them, you can have them done by a surrogate. After all, no one is likely to hold an intermediary's actions against you, particularly if that intermediary is your lawyer. Similarly, when a request is based on the need to get your spouse or significant other to agree to a move, it is likely to be viewed sympathetically. Even if it is not granted, at least you are not likely to be viewed unfavorably for having made the request.

Summary of Negotiating Points

- Treat lawyers and accountants as advisers; don't let them make your decisions for you.

- Negotiate as much of the package as possible yourself before getting lawyers involved.

- Call upon lawyers and accountants to lend credibility or to neutralize company experts.

- Use others to press positions you would not want to argue yourself.

- Use a lawyer to take difficult positions so you can disavow them if the company reacts negatively.

- Place the responsibility on others when you are pressing issues that benefit them.

17

Add-ons: Just One Last Thing

Many things which cannot be overcome when they are together, yield themselves up when taken little by little. PLUTARCH

I recently finished negotiating a labor agreement with a union in Pennsylvania. I was representing a company that needed to get certain concessions from its union in order to survive. Most of its competitors were nonunion companies that paid their employees lower salaries and provided fewer benefits than my client did. The negotiations were long and contentious. We argued about the cost of benefits. We fought over scheduling issues. We argued about the number of sick days employees received. And we disagreed about pay. Medical benefits, however, were the major stumbling block.

After almost six months of negotiating with very little progress, we called in a federal mediator. At about the point when I thought we would never reach an agreement, I met privately with the president of the union and the mediator. With a little creativity we were finally able to come up with a way to resolve the benefits issue. The other issues began to fall into place. As the day went on, we drew close to reaching an agreement. Only two issues remained.

The union wanted us to schedule employees strictly on the basis of seniority, and it also wanted more shop stewards. We could not agree to the scheduling proposal. So we offered to compromise on the number of stewards and agreed to advise our managers to consider seniority when determining schedules. The union representatives considered our proposal for about half an hour. When they returned, their chief negotiator informed us that the union would agree to the deal if the company gave each employee two T-shirts. The company was already providing its employees with workshirts, but the union wanted T-shirts for the summer months. In six months of negotiating the union had never once mentioned T-shirts. Now, at the last minute, it was asking for them in order to close the deal. The company's director of human resources did not want to give the employees T-shirts. Frankly, I didn't want to give them the shirts either.

We had already achieved most of what we wanted. The company would remain competitive. Under the circumstances, the union had received a fair deal. The request for T-shirts, at most, would cost the company a few hundred dollars. We knew we could probably get the same deal without the T-shirts, although it might take another negotiating session. In light of how close we were to a final agreement, and everything we had accomplished, was it worth risking it all over T-shirts that cost a few hundred dollars? Clearly it was not worth jeopardizing a deal that we had worked six months to complete. The union knew it and so did we. In the end we threw in the T-shirts.

There are several lessons to be learned from this story. First, you can usually get the other side to sweeten the deal a little bit as you near the end. If you are not careful, however, that little bit of sweetener can leave a bitter taste in the mouth of your future employer. Thus, although this strategy almost always works, it should be used very carefully. In many cases, it is better not to use it at all. Since this tactic comes into play only as the negotiations are about to be concluded, it should be used, if at all, for something that can be reasonably justified at such a late point in the negotiations. Moreover, this strategy will usually be successful only if the request is neither particularly costly nor problematic for the employer.

If you request something you have not previously discussed, your future employer may feel it is being taken advantage of, even if the company ultimately acquiesces to your demands. Unless a recent development has forced you to raise a new issue at the last minute (perhaps the issue has just arisen or you honestly forgot about it), it is not a good idea to bring up a completely new subject as an "add-on." Rather, it is better to seek to improve upon something you have already been discussing but have yet to finally agree upon.

Let's assume that a prospective employer has offered you its standard relocation package. That relocation policy provides for one trip for you and your spouse to look for a house. Your spouse thinks you will need at least two house-hunting trips. You want the company to pay for the second trip. In response to an offer from the company which resolves most of the outstanding issues, you might say: "I think I could live with that, but I've discussed the move at home and my spouse thinks that we will need at least two house-hunting trips, since we don't know the area at all. Would that be acceptable?" Presented that way, the add-on will usually be agreed to. (See Strategy 16—Blaming the Lawyers, Accountants, and Others.)

A variation of the add-on technique is to seek a minor change in a nonmonetary issue which has not yet been finally resolved. For instance, your prospective employer wants you to sign an "agreement not to compete" in the event you leave the company. You accept the fact that the company will be giving you access to confidential information which it legitimately would not want to fall into the hands of a competitor. By the same token, you want to be able to find another job using your skills when you leave this employer. As a practical matter, your skills are marketable only to a limited number of companies. Your new employer is going to want the agreement not to compete to be written very broadly so that it covers every possible competitor. You, of course, are going to want to narrow the restrictions. If you are not able to resolve this issue to your satisfaction during the negotiations, as they near a conclusion you could condition your acceptance of the offer on the company's agreeing to a more focused definition of whom it considers to be "a competitor." That definition, for example, could be limited to the company's key competitors, excluding those companies that don't compete in its principal areas of business.

An add-on strategy works because once people have invested time and energy in something, they have a psychological need to bring it to a successful conclusion. The longer the parties have been negotiating, the more effective this strategy is. (See Strategy 8—Creating a Stake in the Outcome.) The greater the stake, the more likely people are to agree to a final concession in order to close the deal. If the concession being sought is relatively small, the negotiator almost instinctively will say yes to it. That way the agreement can be concluded without any further waste of the negotiator's time. Unless you appear to be taking undue advantage, the negotiator will generally agree to your request. Even if it is clear that you are trying to take advantage, you may still get what you want. However, that agreement may be achieved at the cost of damaging your future relationship with the negotiator and with your new employer.

As I have stressed throughout this book, honesty is critical to successful negotiations. Unlike most other negotiating techniques, an add-on strategy rarely works well if it is planned ahead of time. If at the beginning of negotiations you tell yourself that you are going to use an add-on technique to try to upgrade the standard company car, the company will recognize what you are doing. Even if you get what you are seeking, the ploy may work to your disadvantage in the long run. Add-ons generally cannot be scripted in advance. Rather, opportunities to request add-ons need to be recognized. If you understand the technique, as the negotiations draw to a close you will be able to ask for add-ons in a way that does not appear to be manipulative.

Another word of caution. Don't try to reopen an issue that the negotiator considers settled. If you've already agreed on a relocation package, don't at the last minute seek to get one more house-hunting trip. It will reflect badly on your integrity. It could even result in the company having second thoughts about its offer. If during the negotiations you are not certain that you want to accept a particular term exactly as it is being proposed, be sure that you keep the issue open for further discussion. A statement such as "I need to think about that" (you anticipate significant changes) or "That generally seems ok but I need to review it further" (you anticipate requesting minor changes) will serve that purpose. Keeping an issue open in this manner enables you to move the negotiations forward, but at the same time allows you to come back to that issue later without causing the other side to feel that you cannot be trusted. As you get close to an overall agreement, you will need to resolve all the outstanding issues. When you get what appears to be the employer's final offer covering all the remaining issues, you can usually persuade the employer to agree to one or two additional items provided they are not major.

What types of issues merit the add-on technique? Only those that will not make your future employer think you are being greedy. Considering whether your request can be justified as job-related is a good test. For instance, any item that will help you do your job better and can be supported on that basis is a good candidate for an add-on. Getting a new computer, bringing along your current secretary, and being given a certain size expense account (if your job requires entertaining clients) could all be justified as last-minute add-ons. Issues needed to satisfy a spouse, such as those related to moving or to finding your spouse a job, are also good candidates to be treated as add-ons. After all, an employer will not blame you for issues that your spouse raises at the last minute, particularly if you have previously indicated that your spouse has some reservations concerning, for instance, relocation. Trying to upgrade the company car that is offered to you, on the other hand, would generally not be appropriate. Other issues that might be suitable subjects to request as add-ons will become apparent during the negotiating process.

Asking for add-ons is much riskier in employment negotiations than it is, for example, in purchasing a car. After all, you don't care what the car dealer thinks of you when you insist that floor mats be thrown into the deal, just as long as you get the floor mats. Not so when you are being hired for a new job. Although the add-on strategy is as effective in employment negotiations as in other types of negotiations, it needs to be used more selectively. Whenever you are tempted to use the strategy, think carefully about how your employer will perceive your request. Is it reasonable? Can you justify it or will the request be viewed as nothing more than an attempt to squeeze a little bit more out of the company? If the company would view such a request as taking advantage, don't ask. You can ill afford to have your new employer view you in that light.

Summary of Negotiating Points

- You can usually get a prospective employer to improve its offer as you get close to an agreement.
- Don't ask for too much.
- Don't ask for something you have not previously discussed unless you have a good reason for bringing it up at the last minute.
- Be reasonable.
- Do not make the company negotiator feel manipulated.
- Take advantage of the fact that the negotiator will ordinarily want to conclude the deal promptly.
- Be careful how you use add-ons in employment negotiations.
- If you have any doubts, don't ask for an add-on.
- Keep in mind that how you negotiate can affect your career.

18

Looking for Exceptions

Any fool can keep a rule. God gave him a
brain to know when to break the rule.
GENERAL WINFIELD SCOTT

A manufacturing executive retained me to represent him in negotiations with a company that was recruiting him to be its chief financial officer. After finding out what was important to him, I checked the company's proxy statement. A proxy statement is a report sent annually by every public company to its shareholders before they elect the company's board of directors. The proxy statement must contain certain information, including a compensation summary of the top five company executives, and must be filed annually with the Securities and Exchange Commission. This particular company's proxy statement included the following footnote in the compensation summary:

> Includes a payment of $45,000 to Mr. Jones to compensate for benefits forgone in connection with his resigning from his prior employer and a payment of $9480 to provide 401(k) plan equivalent benefits for the period prior to Mr. Jones' plan eligibility.

With this information, how difficult do you think it was to get the company to compensate my client for the bonus he was losing by changing jobs and to give him 401(k) equivalent benefits until he became eligible to participate in the plan? That is an example of looking for exceptions.

Fairness and competitiveness in the job market are guiding principles that most employers use in determining whether to provide a certain type of compensation or grant a benefit that is not ordinarily afforded to an employee. Understanding how to use fairness is an essential tool in your negotiating arsenal. (See Principles for Negotiating: The Ten Commandments of Employment Negotiations.) For example, when I suggested that my client be compensated for the money he would lose during the required waiting period before he became eligible to participate in the company's 401(k) plan, the employer readily agreed. I met little resistance, because of the way the request was made. I made sure the company was aware that I knew others had been afforded this benefit. I then pointed out the additional benefits, including his annual bonus, my client was losing because the company wanted him to start as soon as possible. To compensate him for the benefits he had to forgo as a result of leaving his current employer the company agreed to a signing bonus.

Once you have determined that an exception has been made for someone else, you can generally expect to be afforded similar treatment if you ask. The employer's sense of fairness will ordinarily result in acquiescence to your request. If that doesn't work, you can tactfully indicate to the prospective employer that you know others have received the requested benefit. The company's sense of guilt at being caught trying to get away with treating you differently will typically ensure a quick capitulation on the issue.

Be careful how you convey the information you have. You don't want to be accusatory or to back the person you are dealing with into a corner. If you do, that person may feel a need to justify the previous denial of your request. As a result, the negotiator may take the position that your circumstances differ from those in which the company has granted similar benefits in the past.

One way to avoid causing the negotiator to become defensive is by asking a question. (See Strategy 3—Seek and You Shall Find: Tactical Use of Questions.) For instance, you might say, "I have heard that others have been given signing bonuses in the past. Could you check into that? After all, I will be giving up my year-end bonus if I take the job now."

The opposite is also true. If a company has never compensated new hires for the loss of 401(k) benefits during the waiting period before the employees become eligible to participate in the plan, it will be exceedingly difficult to convince the company to do so for you. It will not want to set a precedent which might require those benefits to be granted to future new hires.

When you ask for anything that is not a standard company benefit, you may be confronted with "We couldn't do that; it's not in accordance with company policy." Such a response is typical of someone who is not high up in the company hierarchy. An employee at that level may not even be aware that an exception could be made. Alternatively, the employee may not feel comfortable asking for the authority to do so. Higher-level employees may invoke "company policy" simply because it is convenient or because they are looking for a reason to deny your request.

If the person you are dealing with doesn't have the authority to make an exception or to change the policy, it is usually best to move directly to someone who does. [See Strategy 21—Bypass the Negotiator (Unless It's Your Future Boss).] This strategy is particularly effective if the person with the requisite authority is your new boss.

On the other hand, if "company policy" is invoked because the negotiator wants to avoid dealing with the issue or cannot think of any other reason to justify denying your request, you may want to try convincing this person that it would be inequitable to apply the policy in your situation. Policies are ordinarily promulgated for good reasons. When those reasons don't make sense under the particular circumstances, exceptions can be, and frequently are, made. A policy can also be changed if the rationale for it no longer makes sense or if the circumstances you are faced with were not contemplated when the policy was issued.

Don't let yourself be intimidated by someone who responds to a legitimate request by pointing to "company policy" as if it were a sacred commandment handed down from on high. Ask if the company has ever made an exception to that policy. Suggest that the policy obviously was not meant to apply in your circumstances. Argue that it would be unfair to apply the policy. If all else fails, raise the issue with someone at a higher level.

Relocation is one area where employers are often willing to make exceptions to their standard policy. Typically, relocation policies provide different benefits depending on the employee's level. They include the costs of the physical move (i.e., the costs of the moving company) and closing costs on the purchase of a new home, up to a specified limit. More often than not, a company will agree to a request for a lump-sum payment in lieu of reimbursement for actual relocation expenses—provided that payment is less than the maximum allowed under the relocation policy. A lump-sum payment may be preferable if you don't have much to move and are able to handle the relocation yourself. Alternatively, rather than seeking reimbursement under the company's relocation policy for expenses incurred in connection with the purchase of a new home, you might ask the company to pay for an apartment for a period of time. This approach makes sense for both you and for the company if you are likely to be transferred in one or two years. Other exceptions to the standard relocation package that employers commonly agree to are interest-rate subsidies (if interest rates are high), interest-free loans, loans that become forgivable after an employee has been with the company for a certain period of time, estate-planning advice for employees relocating overseas, temporary living allowances, and the purchase of an employee's home if it cannot be sold within a specified period of time.

Keep in mind that you are not likely to be offered the same relocation package as the company's chief executive officer. However, depending on your circumstances, you may be able to obtain some of those same benefits. For instance, if interest rates are high and you currently have a mortgage with a low interest rate, it is reasonable to ask for an interest-rate subsidy for a period of time or for the company to pay "points" in order to reduce the amount you will have to pay in monthly mortgage payments. Typically, companies will pay from one to three points, depending on local custom and practice. The fact that the company recently gave similar benefits to another employee, even if that employee was at a higher level, can still be used to your advantage. In all probability, the reason the company agreed to provide those benefits applies equally to your situation, even if the overall amount is scaled down to reflect the level of your job. If you are dealing with a benefit such as an interest subsidy or points, the cost of that benefit will usually already reflect the salary and level of your new position, because the cost to the company will be based on the price of the home being purchased.

Another area where exceptions are commonly made is in the area of medical benefits. Employers today often require a waiting period before an employee is eligible to participate in the company's medical plan. During this waiting period most employees exercise their COBRA rights and pay the required premiums to remain in their prior employer's medical plan. You can often get a company to agree to reimburse you for those premium payments.

Where can you find out if certain benefits have been afforded to other employees? As mentioned earlier, the proxy statement of a public corporation will contain a great deal of useful information. This is a public document which can be obtained from the Securities and Exchange Commission and that is now readily available on the Internet as well. (See Getting Ready to Negotiate.)

The idea is to learn everything you can about any special deals that have been made in the past. Current and former employees may also be knowledgeable about what the company has previously done in order to recruit new employees. If all else fails, you can always ask your prospective employer directly whether others have been provided the benefit you are seeking.

Once you determine what special treatment has been afforded to others, you will be in a better position to obtain those same benefits by making the case that your situation is similar. Therefore identifying the exceptions that have been made for others in the organization will give you a critical negotiating advantage.

Summary of Negotiating Points

- Try to find out what special arrangements have been made for new hires in the past.
- Seek those same benefits to the extent that they are appropriate to your circumstances.
- Issues related to relocation are particularly susceptible to special arrangements.
- Reimbursement for COBRA payments if the company's medical plan has a waiting period is common.
- Bear in mind that your prospective employer will be guided by fairness and market conditions.
- The level of the position you are being hired for will likely have an impact on what exceptions the company is willing to make.
- Don't be intimidated by someone who responds to a legitimate request by invoking "company policy."
- Policies can be changed and exceptions can be made.

19
Using Headhunters When You Negotiate

Filling jobs is the objective; accommodating executives is not.

JOHN LUCHT (ON EXECUTIVE RECRUITERS)

Larry had been working with an executive search firm that was conducting a search for a vice president of operations. He had completed the interview process and emerged as the company's top candidate. Late one Monday afternoon the recruiter called Larry to inform him of that fact and to set up a meeting with the company. She now began to question Larry about the details of his current compensation, a subject he had managed to deal with in generalities up to this point. Larry continued to avoid directly answering her questions. (See Strategy 1—Making the Most of Your Compensation: Discussing Your Current Salary.) Instead, he asked the recruiter what the company was thinking about in terms of compensation. She responded that she didn't exactly know but that it had mentioned a salary in the $75,000 to $100,000 range. Larry told her that he was expecting something in the $100,000 range. (Moments earlier, he had been thinking that an $85,000 salary would be acceptable!) Then he thanked the recruiter for all her help and set up an appointment to meet with his future boss the next day.

What Larry was able to do was to use the headhunter both to get information and to send a message to the company about his salary expectations. Those are two ways you can make use of a recruiter during the negotiating process. Keep in mind, however, that the executive recruiter is being paid by the employer. The company will probably be trying to use the recruiter in the same way. It will be trying to have the recruiter get information from you, about both your current compensation and your expectations. The company will also be using the recruiter to get feedback about its proposals. As a result, you generally will not get any information from the recruiter that the company does not want you to have.

If you are using the recruiter to channel information to the company and it is using the recruiter to channel information to you, why not simply talk directly to each other? In the first place, sometimes one party to the negotiations, usually the job candidate, does not understand the role the recruiter is playing in the negotiating process; the other party will gain a significant advantage as a result. If, for example, a recruiter is able to get you to provide a detailed breakdown of your current compensation and benefit package, the company will know exactly what it needs to pay in order to put together an attractive offer. Similarly, once you tell the recruiter what you are looking for, you can be certain that a prospective employer will not offer you more than that, regardless of what it might have offered in the absence of that information.

Even if each side understands the role recruiters play in the process, they can still serve a beneficial purpose. A recruiter can be used to feel the other side out on various issues. By raising an issue through the recruiter, you can avoid locking yourself into a fixed position that would be difficult to back down from. This is often the most important role an executive recruiter can play in the negotiating process. Maxine Hartley, a highly regarded executive recruiter with Pearl Management L.L.C. in New York, advises candidates who work with recruiters to negotiate through them. According to Maxine:

> Because ego is frequently involved during the negotiation of sensitive issues such as compensation, title, and responsibilities, rarely should a candidate negotiate directly with the company if a recruiter is involved. Once an ill-conceived comment or request has been made by the candidate, it cannot be undone. The candidate is damaged, sometimes irreparably. The headhunter can effectively serve as a lightning rod, advocating the candidate's position without jeopardizing his or her candidacy.

A recruiter can also strengthen your bargaining position by noting that you are being sought after by other companies. A recruiter can do this more easily and with greater credibility than you can.

One of my clients, whom I will call Amanda, was being considered for a position as executive vice president for a publishing company. The company had used an executive recruiter to conduct the search. Now that Amanda had been selected for the position, the recruiter was seeking to get information for the company about her expectations. After some small talk, the conversation went something like this:

RECRUITER: What would it take for them to be able to convince you to join the company?

AMANDA: I would want a base of between $100,000 and $125,000, depending on what the company is offering in terms of stock options and bonus.

RECRUITER: I think $125,000 is a little high for them.

AMANDA: Then we should probably discuss bonus and stock options. Do they have a bonus plan for executives at my level?

RECRUITER: I don't know. Why don't you ask them when you meet with them on Thursday?

AMANDA: I'd appreciate it if you can get me that information before the meeting so that I can be prepared to discuss it intelligently.

Amanda used the recruiter very effectively. First, by giving a range in response to the recruiter's question about her expectations, she presented the company with some general parameters but retained a great deal of negotiating flexibility. In fact, what she did was to determine where the bidding will start. Normally a company will offer the minimum salary that is suggested in order to leave itself room to negotiate. It can then gauge the candidate's reaction to what is being offered, and respond accordingly. Therefore, if you suggest a range of acceptable salaries, make sure you are comfortable with the lowest salary you suggest. Eventually you may be able to get the company to offer you more, but that is always difficult. Moreover, if the company does subsequently increase its salary offer, it will usually be at the expense of something else you want.

By specifically conditioning her willingness to accept a certain salary on the number of stock options being offered and her potential bonus, Amanda left herself free to ask for additional salary, a larger bonus, more stock options, or some combination thereof. This approach sets the stage for further discussions after the company makes its initial proposal. The discussions will focus on possible trade-offs among base salary, bonus, and stock options. (See Strategy 10—Be Flexible: Consider the Possibilities.) Unfortunately, the bonus and particularly the stock options that were actually offered to Amanda were less than she had hoped for. Even after persuading the company to increase its salary offer to $110,000, she felt that she should be able to get more.

Amanda then switched to a strategy that is very effective when negotiating through a recruiter. She floated several "trial balloons." She indicated that she was very interested in the job but was disappointed with the stock option package being offered. She asked if there was any way the company could increase the number of options. After speaking with the company, the recruiter informed her that it couldn't. She then asked if, in light of that, the recruiter thought it would be reasonable for her to ask for a signing bonus. After all, by leaving her company before year end, Amanda was giving up her bonus and the company match to her 401(k) plan. The recruiter acknowledged that the request was not unreasonable, but she did not know if the company would agree. She offered to find out. In the end, the company did agree to a signing bonus and Amanda accepted the job.

Floating trial balloons is one way to use a recruiter. You can explore various options through the recruiter without committing yourself to any specific proposal and without losing credibility if the company is not willing to consider what you are suggesting. By so doing, you can also enlist the recruiter as your advocate. One way to float a trial balloon is to raise the issue first with the recruiter: "The company's offer provides for six months' severance. I am concerned about the possibility that the company may be taken over and feel a year's severance would be appropriate. Do you think the company would agree to that?" By working through the recruiter, you leave yourself room to back away from a particular position if the company does not respond positively.

In addition to floating trial balloons, you can use the recruiter as an outlet for expressing your concern or displeasure with a particular proposal. Those comments will be viewed very differently than if you made them directly to the company. You might even suggest to the recruiter that, unless a particular issue is resolved to your satisfaction, you cannot see any way to accept the offer. You would almost never make such a comment directly to the company negotiator.

Finally, you can always ask for the recruiter's help, particularly when you have reached an impasse on a difficult issue. You can describe the problem to the recruiter and solicit ideas as to how to resolve it. After all, the recruiter knows the company better than you do and should have a good idea of what is possible. An executive recruiter can explore various alternatives with the company in a way that you could not. When the recruiter discusses an idea with the company, it is not a proposal from someone they are negotiating with. It is a suggestion from someone who is working for the company. Moreover, if the recruiter is the one suggesting the solution, he or she will generally work hard to convince the employer. The fact that it comes from the recruiter, rather than from you, makes it more likely that the company will accept the proposal as well.

Executive recruiters have a significant incentive to ensure the successful completion of the negotiations. They have a major stake in the outcome. If they are hired on a contingency fee basis, they get paid only if their candidate accepts the job. Even if the recruiter is hired on a retainer basis and gets paid regardless of whether any particular candidate accepts the job, if you turn down the job, the recruiter must spend time and effort to find another candidate acceptable to the company. In either case, the recruiter has an incentive to try to help the parties reach an agreement. Knowing that, you can use the recruiter to advance your negotiating agenda.

Summary of Negotiating Points

- Use the recruiter to get information.
- Assume that any information you get from the recruiter is information that the company wants you to have.
- Provide information to the recruiter that you would like conveyed to the company.
- Use the recruiter to float trial balloons.
- Use the recruiter as an avenue to express unhappiness with a proposal.
- Ask the recruiter for help when you have reached an impasse.
- Always remember that the recruiter is being paid by the company.

20

Making the Company Negotiator Look Good

The deepest principle of human nature is the craving to be appreciated.   WILLIAM JAMES

Several years ago, an executive hired me to handle the negotiations when he was recruited to become chief operating officer of a growing technology company. The company was being represented by its regular outside corporate counsel. The negotiations were extremely difficult. We went back and forth on almost every point. Mostly we negotiated with each other by phone, exchanging written proposals by fax and calling our clients as necessary. Sometimes weeks would go by before the company's attorney would get back to me on a particular point.

The company's lawyer was a very good negotiator and clearly understood the significance of every word and comma that we agreed upon. However, I thought he frequently missed chances to put his client at an advantage. He was so focused on ensuring that the contract language we agreed to was exactly the way he wanted it that substantively he often gave up more than he needed to. He obviously was proud of his skills as a draftsman. I was able to get significant concessions by agreeing to the language he was proposing on issues that were not of major concern to my client. As you can imagine, this was a long and painstaking process.

Suddenly, however, my adversary began to be more accommodating. We quickly reached agreement on a number of issues. I knew that I would be able to get most of what my client wanted on the remaining issues. Up to that point I was getting what I wanted by allowing the company's counsel to determine how certain contract language would be written. Now I recognized that his agenda had changed. He obviously had been told to get the deal done. When he learned that I was going away on Friday morning for a long weekend, the pace quickened even more. When by the end of the business day Thursday we still had not finished and I suggested we talk on Monday, he clearly was concerned. He asked if we could try to wrap things up that night. I knew that if I agreed, it would increase my bargaining leverage, because I could always threaten to break off the negotiations and get back to him when I returned the following week. Also, I had grown to like this fellow and understood that if I took off for the weekend before we concluded, he would have a problem with his client. So we kept working until we finished. My client was happy; I think his client was happy. By understanding his needs and allowing him to look good with his client, I got the best deal possible for mine. Later I found out that the reason for the sudden urgency was that the company was eager to announce the appointment. In fact, the lawyer had been told to get the deal done so my client could tell his boss and an announcement could be made on Monday.

The best way to be successful in your negotiations is to understand the agenda of the person you are dealing with. Keep in mind that the negotiator's interests may not be the same as those of the company. The negotiator may want to conclude the negotiations quickly because of another project that needs attention. Or the negotiator may be under instructions to make sure that you accept the job offer. Alternatively, that individual may be under strict budgetary constraints, limiting what can be offered. Whatever the negotiator's agenda, you will be more successful if you understand it

Letting the negotiator look good in ways that do not cost you a great deal will make it easier for you to negotiate. How do you find out what the other side's agenda is? Usually all you have to do is listen carefully to what is being said. Get the negotiator to talk about his or her job. Watch body language. An experienced negotiator will not reveal the company's bottom line. He or she is, however, likely to provide subtle signals as to the company's priorities. In addition, the negotiator will feel much freer about discussing the things that he or she is involved in, since they will not have a direct impact on the negotiations. These topics may give you some indication of the negotiator's personal priorities.

Finding out to whom this person must answer may give you some insight into what the negotiator needs to do to look good in the eyes of the boss. For example, if the negotiator reports to the chief financial officer, the total cost of the package may be the primary concern. Since stock options have no impact on a company's current earnings, an individual reporting to the chief financial officer may be more willing to increase the number of stock options you are granted than to increase the amount of a signing bonus. On the other hand, if the boss is the head of sales and marketing, getting you on board quickly may be of paramount importance. If the negotiator is from the human resources area or the legal department, the boss may be primarily interested in the impact your deal will have on others in the organization.

The person you are negotiating with will also want to be thought well of by you. This is particularly true if you are dealing with your future boss. You can take advantage of that person's self-image. If you are dealing with a seasoned veteran, the negotiator may want to demonstrate to you how good a company this is to work for. A boss who fancies himself a mentor will want to help you negotiate a good deal. Seek his help. Someone who fancies herself a teacher will want to share knowledge about the company with you. Encourage her to do so. Most people consider themselves to be fair. Appeals to fairness, therefore, will be effective with most of the people you negotiate with in the employment context—with one notable exception. Most lawyers and business executives are competitive. Some, however, carry this trait to an extreme. Appeals to fairness will generally be less effective with these types. It is more important to let them believe that they have "outnegotiated" you.

The lawyer who represented the technology company during the negotiations described above fell neatly into this category. He not only considered himself a craftsman but needed to "win" points during the negotiations. You need to allow these people to "win." You don't, however, have to give up things that are important to do so. (See Strategy 15—Creating Red Herring Issues.) Let them win on the issues you select. Reluctantly give in on issues you don't consider of major importance. By understanding what your goals really are, you will know which issues to concede on. Periodically referring to the list of goals you created in preparing for the negotiations will keep you on track when you are tempted to concede on an important issue without receiving something of equal value in return. (See Strategy 11—Patience, Persistence, and Timing: Outmaneuvering or Outlasting Your Opponent.)

Understanding and helping your adversary obtain his or her objectives, while at the same time achieving your own goals will generally enable you to negotiate a better deal. (See Strategy 5—Creating a Win-Win Situation.) The more successful you are, the more important it is to make sure the person you are bargaining with feels good about the outcome. This is particularly true if you are negotiating with your future boss. When the negotiations are over, compliment the other side about the way the negotiations were handled. Say nice things about the company's negotiator to someone who will tell him. Let his boss know how professionally the negotiations were handled.'

Finally, you should make it easy for the negotiator to agree with you. Sometimes she will want to agree but won't want to look like she is giving in. She may be under pressure to agree to what you want in order to complete the negotiations quickly and may resent that fact. Let her save face. Don't box her into a corner. Concede on a minor point. Agree reluctantly. Let her choose among options which are equally favorable to you. (See Strategy 10—Be Flexible: Consider the Possibilities.) Always make sure that the company negotiator believes she got the best deal possible under the circumstances.

Summary of Negotiating Points

- Understand the agenda of the person you are negotiating with.
- Remember that the negotiator may have an agenda which differs from that of the company.
- Try to find out to whom the negotiator must answer and help that individual look good in the boss's eyes.
- Take advantage of the negotiator's self-image.
- Make it easy for the company negotiator to agree with you.
- Make sure the people you are dealing with feel good about the outcome of the negotiations.

21

Bypass the Negotiator (Unless It's Your Future Boss)

I don't want to talk to Jerry Mahoney, I want to talk to Paul Winchell.
    HOWARD STERN (REFERRING TO A STAGE DUMMY
                    AND A VENTRILOQUIST)

Since I graduated from law school, I have purchased four new cars and leased one. Except for the car I bought for my 18-year-old son, I negotiated very good deals on each of those purchases. (You lose all bargaining leverage if you make the mistake of bringing an 18-year-old buying his first car along with you.) I learned something from each of these negotiations.

One important lesson I learned is that you don't negotiate with anyone who does not have the authority to give you what you want. Typically when you buy a new car, the salesperson has no authority to agree to anything. The salesperson negotiates with you and then announces, "I have to take what you just agreed to back to my sales manager for approval." Then the sales manager comes out and tries to renegotiate everything you have already agreed upon. This is a very effective negotiating tactic. If you don't know it is going to happen, you will have already given away too much before the real bargaining begins. You will also have the disadvantage of having a psychological stake in reaching an agreement after you invested time and energy in bargaining with the salesperson. The sales manager, on the other hand, has just come into the process and will be in a stronger bargaining position. (See Strategy 8—Creating a Stake in the Outcome.)

You need to be aware that most car dealers will try to use this tactic on you. Similarly, when you are engaged in employment negotiations, you want to make sure that you are bargaining with someone who has sufficient authority. Sometimes, however, that may be problematic. If bypassing a lower-level negotiator will damage relationships that may be important to your future career with the company, it may be better to work through that person even if it means that the negotiations will be more difficult.

There are three basic situations, however, when you should consider trying to bypass the negotiator: (1) when the negotiator has no authority, (2) when the negotiator is using lack of authority as a negotiating tactic, and (3) when the negotiator has the authority to agree but is not willing to do so. Your response to each of these situations will vary. However, your goal in each instance will be to negotiate with someone other than the person you are dealing with. As the title of this chapter indicates, if you are bargaining with your future boss it will be hard, and probably ill advised, to try to end-run that individual in order to negotiate with someone else. Attempting to do so is likely to damage your relationship and most likely your career as well.

After you have successfully completed the company's interview process, the normal practice is for someone from the human resources department to get back to you with an offer. This person will often be the recruiter who first contacted you about the position. (In smaller companies the human resources director or your future boss may handle the follow-up directly.) If you are offered the job by someone other than your future boss, that person will be able to convey the terms of the offer, explain company benefits, and answer any questions you may have. However, someone in that position generally will not have the authority to negotiate further or modify the terms of the offer. The response you will likely receive is "I am not in a position to do anything about that" or "Let me get back to you." Often some reference will be made to company policy or to how "we don't do that here."

Once you have determined that this person has no real ability to agree to anything of importance, you have several options. First, you can try to find out who has the necessary authority and speak to that person directly. Second, you can seek assistance from your new boss. Finally, if you choose to, or have no choice but to, you can work through the lower-level person and make concessions sparingly. Understand that whatever you agree to may be subject to renegotiation by someone else.

When you are dealing with someone who lacks authority, try to discuss the less important issues first in order to get a feel for how to negotiate with this person. Preliminary discussion may also provide you with an excuse to deal with someone else. If, for example, you are told that the company would not approve something that you thought the negotiator had previously agreed to, find out who was responsible for that decision. Then try to speak directly with that person or ask your future boss to intervene. Another approach when dealing with someone who does not have sufficient authority is to request that the company propose solutions to the issues you raise. It is exceedingly difficult for people to claim that they cannot agree to something if they are the ones who propose it. Finally, you can make your proposals tentative as well. For example, you might tell the person you are dealing with that what you are suggesting is subject to change after you have had the opportunity to review it with your lawyer, accountant, or spouse. (See Strategy 16—Blaming the Lawyers, Accountants, and Others.)

You can use the same responses if you are dealing with someone who you believe actually has authority to reach a final agreement, at least within certain limits, but purports to need someone else's approval for whatever you agree upon. This is a position that lawyers like to take. Lawyers understand how to use the claim of lack of authority to their client's advantage. They typically are given sufficient authority to reach an agreement, or at least they have a very good understanding of what their client is willing to agree to. To be able to claim a lack of authority, many lawyers will actually ask their clients not to give them certain authority. That way they can truthfully state that they need to discuss your proposals with their client before they can agree to anything.

There are several other ways to respond to a feigned claim of lack of authority. One is to seek to embarrass the negotiator into "getting" the appropriate authority by suggesting that it might be easier if you dealt directly with the person making the decisions. Another way to level the playing field, particularly if the company's attorney is claiming a lack of authority, is to bring your own attorney into the process. Your lawyer will, of course, be equally limited in authority. Alternatively, you can try to negotiate the substantive aspects of the agreement directly with your future boss or with someone else at the company who has sufficient authority, leaving the "drafting of the agreement" to the lawyers.

When the company's lawyer is involved, it is relatively easy to take the position that you do not feel comfortable without your own attorney

also being present. You can then suggest speaking directly with someone at the company in the interest of time. In the unusual situation
where your future employer still wants its lawyer to handle the discussions, it is not unreasonable to ask that the company pay your attorney's
fees. Finally, when you have to deal with someone who uses lack of
authority as a negotiating tactic, be wary of agreeing to any major concessions before you have obtained a firm commitment from the company as to what it is willing to do in return.

The most difficult and possibly most beneficial situation in which to
bypass the person you are negotiating with arises when that person
actually has the necessary authority but is not willing to agree to what
you want. When this occurs, you have to find a way to raise the issue
with someone at a higher level without unnecessarily antagonizing the
person you are negotiating with. Even if the second person is not at a
higher level, he or she may still have sufficient influence to change the
negotiator's position. If you are negotiating with people from human
resources or the legal department, for instance, they will generally be
very solicitous of the wishes of line managers for fear of being accused
of insensitivity to the needs of the business.

Typically, the person you seek out in attempting to bypass the negotiator will be your future boss. That individual has the most at stake in
your accepting the company's offer and is the logical person to cham-
pion your cause. It is only natural to discuss a problem that might prevent you from joining the company with the executive who is hiring
you. However, even if your future boss is at a higher level than the original negotiator, you need to approach the situation carefully. If you ask
your prospective boss to overrule the negotiator, even if your boss is in
a position to do so, he or she may choose not to. Your new boss may
believe it is not the right thing to do or may want to avoid causing inter-
nal problems. Similarly, the person being overruled may seek support
from his or her boss or may otherwise attempt to sabotage the deal.
Even if the original negotiator is forced to agree, you could be creating
an enemy who is in a position to damage your career at some future
date. Therefore it is better to seek help in getting someone to influence
rather than try to overrule the negotiator. One possible approach is to
describe the problem to your prospective boss and seek advice on how
to handle the situation. Ask if there is anything the boss can do to help.
Once your future boss agrees to get involved, the issue is likely to be
resolved in your favor.

What should you do if your future boss is the one making the offer
and doesn't have sufficient authority, pretends not to have authority, or
has the authority to agree but won't? Do the best you can and negotiate
anyway, unless you can get your future boss to suggest that you speak

with someone else. Although there is no sure-fire way to get your boss to do that, there are ways you can encourage it. For example, if your prospective boss blames an impasse on company policy, ask if there is someone you could talk to who would be able to make an exception to the policy. If the boss does not refer you elsewhere, you will just have to live with what is being offered or not accept the job. (See Strategy 25— Walking Away.) It is a Pyrrhic victory to get what you want by making your new boss feel that you went over his or her head to get it. It is unlikely that the boss will ever trust you. That is clearly not the way to start off a new relationship.

Summary of Negotiating Points

- If possible, avoid negotiating with anyone who doesn't have authority to agree to what you want.

- If you have to negotiate with someone who doesn't have sufficient authority, make concessions sparingly.

- If you are negotiating with someone who lacks sufficient authority, get the company to propose ways to resolve your concerns.

- If the person you are dealing with is using a lack of authority as a negotiating tactic, consider having someone else negotiate for you.

- If you need to bypass the negotiator, appeal to your future boss for help.

- Be especially careful how you handle someone who has the authority to agree to what you want but won't do so. Seek to influence rather than overrule.

- If your future boss is doing the negotiating, never go over his or her head without permission.

22

Using Information: Facts, Figures, and Comparisons

The facts, ma'am. Just the facts.
JACK WEBB IN DRAGNET

Ken was in a tough position. He wanted the job but felt that he was worth more than he was being offered. An expert in distribution, he had worked his way up to be transportation manager in charge of distribution for a large manufacturing company. Because he had been with this company for virtually his whole career, his salary had not kept pace with that of his peers elsewhere. He made the mistake of telling the recruiter exactly what he was earning. (See Strategy 1—Making the Most of Your Compensation: Discussing Your Current Salary.) The offer Ken received was just enough more than he was making to make it worthwhile for him to move but still less than the market rate for comparable jobs.

Ken told the person extending the offer how interested he was in the job and how excited he was about the possibility of joining the company. He conveyed his thanks for the offer but expressed disappointment about the salary. He thought it was low in light of what others in similar positions were earning and offered to provide the company with salary survey data showing what comparably sized companies were paying their transportation managers. In addition, Ken explained how much money he had been able to save his current employer by making the distribution system faster, more efficient, and less costly. In the end, he was able to get the company to agree to a salary and bonus structure more in line with what he considered to be his true market worth.

There are two types of information you can use to negotiate your compensation: information about the market value of the position and information about the value you bring to the position. If people in similar positions at comparable companies earn more than you are being offered, or if they participate in company stock option plans and you won't, you can present that information to your future employer. This data will be very useful if the company is unaware of the market conditions. This frequently happens when the person you are replacing had been with the company for a long time and as a result was being paid a below-market salary. Perhaps that is the reason your predecessor left the company. Moreover, to the extent that you can show your market value because you have another offer, you can usually get the company to improve its offer. (See Strategy 13—Using Another Offer Even When You Don't Have One.)

Often, however, a company that is offering a below-market salary is aware of that fact and is doing so intentionally. Sometimes the company will include something else of equal value as part of its proposal, such as stock. At other times it will offer less than the market rate because it cannot afford to pay more or because paying more would upset the company's salary structure. In that case, you will not be able to use facts about the job market to improve your bargaining position.

Under those circumstances, rely on facts and figures to sell what you can do for the company. How much did you increase sales in your unit last year? How much did you reduce distribution costs? Demonstrate in concrete financial terms to your prospective employer what you were able to accomplish at your prior job. By showing the value you can bring to the company, you are in a better position to get the company to pay you more. After all, if you can demonstrate that you will be able to save a half a million dollars by improving inventory controls as you did for your current employer, it is unlikely that the company will refuse to pay you the extra $10,000 a year you are seeking.

Providing objective, verifiable information to support your position serves other purposes as well. It tends to depersonalize disagreements. Objective data can refocus the parties on the fairness of the proposal. Most important, providing information which supports your position affords the company negotiator a graceful way to give in without losing face. (See Strategy 20—Making the Company Negotiator Look Good.)

Often during negotiations one party will argue so strongly for a position that it is difficult to modify that position even after there is a clear need to do so. New information will allow the negotiator to change his or her stance without appearing to concede. Often that is enough to break what appears to be a serious impasse.

Market data can also be effective when you are in an otherwise weak bargaining position. If, like Ken, you really want the job and are willing to accept the position even though the compensation being offered is not what you expected, objective data showing the value of the position offers your best chance of getting the company to improve its proposal. Employers, no matter how strong their bargaining position, still want to appear to be fair. (See Principles for Negotiating: The Ten Commandments of Employment Negotiations.) When you ask even the most ruthless negotiators about how they treat their employees, they will almost always describe themselves as "tough but fair." Offering objective data to support your position appeals to a need to be fair. Moreover, the company will want you to feel good about joining them, and that will be hard to do if they simply ignore the information you have provided.

Facts, figures, and comparisons—of both market data and the value you bring to your position—can also be useful when you are negotiating with your current employer. Showing what you have accomplished for the company in terms of additional earnings or cost savings is helpful if you are attempting to justify why you deserve a raise. Market rates are also very compelling when you are seeking a salary increase from your current employer. If you are being paid less than others in similar positions, fairness dictates that your employer adjust your salary accordingly. You should also be prepared to show, in concrete terms, how much it would take to train your replacement and how much productivity would be lost as a result. If that still does not do the trick, your employer either does not seriously believe that you might leave or does not care. In either case, you probably should look for another job, if for no other reason than to prove to yourself that you are marketable. Once you have another offer, you can use that to negotiate a salary increase if you still want to remain with your current employer. (See Strategy 13— Using Another Offer Even When You Don't Have One.)

Even information that arguably does not support your stance can be used to your advantage. If there is an obvious weakness in your position, address it. If you don't, the company negotiator certainly will. By bringing it up yourself, you will enhance your credibility. Candor can be disarming. When attorneys try cases, they always want to bring out any problems with their case before the other side does. That way it does not undermine their case. Nobody thinks that you have been caught trying to put something over on them.

Similarly, in all employment negotiations, it is best to directly address any problems with your position. Let's say your new job requires a move to Singapore. In addition to an increase in salary attributable to the additional responsibilities of the job, you have asked that the company take into account the substantially higher cost of living there. Accordingly, you would like the company to provide you not only with a housing allowance but also with an even larger salary increase than it had proposed. In making that request, you would be wise to admit that there are tax advantages to working overseas. After acknowledging that fact, you can then argue that the tax advantages don't offset the high cost of living in Singapore. This will take the argument away from the company negotiator.

Your candor will create trust. It will allow you to develop a relationship with the company negotiator. When you do that, it will be much harder for the company to be less than forthright with you. The more of a personal relationship you develop, the better the deal you will be able to negotiate.

This does not, of course, mean that you should make the company's case for it. Your purpose is to argue forcefully for your proposals, which should be expansive but reasonable. (See Strategy 2—Asking for More Money: You Can't Get It If You Don't Ask.) Only when the employer is certain to raise an objection should you try to preempt it by bringing the issue up first.

Information is critical to the success of any employment negotiations. That is why preparation is so important. (See Getting Ready to Negotiate.) You can use much of the information obtained during your preparation, such as the company's salary structure, to formulate your proposals without ever revealing that you are aware of this information. However, you should provide your prospective employer with other types of verifiable data, such as market surveys and what you have accomplished for your prior employers, in order to support your positions. Even more important, such information can offer the company a justification for changing its position, without having to appear simply to be caving in to your demands.

Summary of Negotiating Points

- There are two types of objective information which can be used to negotiate your compensation: market data and the special value you bring to the position.

- Both types of information can be used effectively when you have a weak bargaining position.

- Objective, verifiable data of either type can be used to support an appeal to fairness.

- Facts, figures, and comparisons can also be particularly useful when you are negotiating with your current employer.

- Providing new information allows the negotiator to give in without losing face.

- Even information that arguably does not support your position can be used to your advantage, provided you bring it out first in order to preempt the argument being raised by the other side.

23

Silence Is Golden: When to Let the Other Side Talk

When you have nothing to say, say nothing.
CHARLES CALEB COLTON

Sandy had been offered a position as advertising director for a specialty store chain. She and her future employer were able to agree on most of the employment terms. The one area in which they were having difficulty reaching agreement involved the severance package. Because of the number of retailers that had gone out of business or been taken over, Sandy was particularly concerned about severance. She had two problems with the employer's offer: the amount of the severance and the fact that the company was insisting that its severance obligation be "mitigated" by any salary earned elsewhere during the severance period.

Mitigation is a legal concept that more and more companies are incorporating into their severance policies. Under a severance arrangement which requires mitigation, severance is paid in the form of salary continuation, with the company reducing the amount of severance by any salary earned elsewhere during the period of continuation. The reason normally given for requiring mitigation is that the purpose of severance is financial protection until employees find other jobs, not to provide them with a windfall. The problem with mitigation is that it reduces or eliminates the incentive to find another job and does not take into account the fact that it may take years for the employee to return to the same salary level following termination.

Sandy had asked for a severance of twelve months' salary to be paid in a lump sum in the event that she was terminated without cause. The company responded by offering to guarantee her six months' salary continuation, mitigated by any salary she earned from another employer during this period. She felt that six months was not sufficient and that her severance should not be reduced if she found other employment. The company's position was that its severance policy included a mitigation provision and it applied to everyone. She was then asked how much severance she would require if it included mitigation. Sandy did not know how to respond to this question. Had she answered, she would have been implicitly accepting the fact that her severance would require mitigation, and the company would then begin negotiating the amount of severance.

Instinctively Sandy understood that when you don't have a good response, don't respond. After pausing for a moment, she turned the question back to the company: "I really had never considered that the severance would require mitigation. Why don't you see how much severance you can provide without mitigation?" (See Strategy 3—Seek and You Shall Find: The Tactical Use of Questions.) About a day later she heard from the company. Sandy was told once more that the employer had to require mitigation because every other executive's severance included mitigation. Then Sandy was again asked what she needed in terms of a severance package if it included mitigation. Sandy responded that she would think it over and get back to the company.

Sandy was not happy with a severance package that required mitigation, but she understood that if all the other executives, without exception, were required to accept it as part of their severance she would probably have to accept a similar arrangement. So she determined to try to protect herself from the possibility of a period of unemployment, or more likely underemployment, by getting more money up front. (See Strategy 10—Be Flexible: Consider the Possibilities.) Sandy recognized that making such a request this late in the negotiations could cause problems. She also knew that the company was anxious to fill the position and that she was the only candidate the employer was considering at that moment. So she simply waited. After about a week she received a call from the executive recruiter who was handling the search. The recruiter wanted to know where things stood. Sandy responded that she didn't know where to go from there. She explained that she had not expected the company to insist on mitigation and was concerned that if she lost her job because of a takeover, her career might be significantly set back. She assumed that, in light of what she knew about the company's severance policy, the most she could expect was a year and with mitigation she did not think that offered her sufficient protection. Sandy then inquired as to whether the recruiter thought a signing bonus was possible. (See Strategy 19—Using the Headhunter to Help You Negotiate.) That way, in the event that she lost her job following a takeover, she at least would have the bonus money to help tide her over. The recruiter offered to find out. In the end, Sally agreed to twelve months' severance with mitigation and a signing bonus.

No one can be certain that Sandy's not calling back for a week made the company more open to her suggestion of a signing bonus than it would have been if she had immediately proposed that solution. However, silence can often work to your advantage during negotiations. Often, if you have stated your position clearly or if you don't like the direction the negotiations are taking, it is best not to say anything more. Let the other side make the next move.

If you are being pressed during negotiations for a response and don't know what to do, find a reason to take a break. Go to the bathroom. Get a cup of coffee. Break for lunch. Indicate that you have to be somewhere and schedule another session. Use the time to regroup. Seek advice. Collect additional information to support your position. Rethink your stance. Develop a new game plan. Let the other side worry about what you are thinking. What is important is to regain control over the pace and the agenda.

One of the most difficult things to do during negotiations is simply to keep quiet and wait. It takes a certain amount of self-assurance simply to make your point and remain silent until the person you are dealing with responds. We are trained from an early age to avoid silence during conversations. Good conversationalists keep the conversation going. Silence makes people uncomfortable. Therefore, if you don't say anything, chances are whomever you are talking to will.

One of the tricks that lawyers use in questioning a witness is to remain silent after the witness completes an answer rather than ask another question. This tactic prompts the witness to continue speaking and often yields more information than was originally provided. Try an experiment with a friend. Ask a general question. After your friend answers, remain silent and continue to look right at him or her. Even if it appears that the speaker was finished, after a brief pause the speaker will inevitably continue with the answer. This technique works equally well during negotiations. Just as nature abhors a vacuum, people are uncomfortable with silence. They will seek to fill the void. For this reason, it is often best to let the other side make the next move. If you say nothing, in all probability the person you are bargaining with will do something to try to move the negotiations forward.

A well-timed delay in getting back to the employer can often work to your advantage, provided you do not appear to be avoiding the company. For the same reason that periods of silence during a conversation create discomfort, breaks in negotiations which last longer than expected, and in which the other side is not heard from, can be unnerving. The company will wonder whether you are still interested or whether you have gotten another offer. It may be under pressure to fill the position quickly. As long as you have not promised to respond by a specific time, you can delay getting back to the company. That could be for a day or it could be for a week, depending on the nature of the negotiations. If you don't schedule a resumption in the bargaining relatively promptly, in all likelihood someone from the company will contact you. How quickly they do will give you some indication as to how anxious they are to complete the negotiations. If they don't contact you within a reasonable period of time, you can always call them. If they ask you why you haven't gotten back to the company, you can respond that you didn't have any good ideas as to how to resolve the problem. Usually this response not only will be truthful but will put the burden on the company to try to come up with a solution.

How should you respond if someone uses these techniques with you? If, while you are negotiating, someone remains silent for a lengthy period of time after you have completed an answer, the best response is for you to pause long enough to make clear that you know what is going on and then ask: "Did that answer your question?" If the company indicates that it will get back to you with a response and doesn't, it is often best to simply wait until it does. If you can't wait, you can call the company, reiterate that you are very interested in the job, and then try to create a sense of urgency. For example, you could state: "I need to get the matter resolved quickly because I have some projects at my current job which would not be fair to start if I plan to leave the company." Or you could ask for a prompt response because you "are also talking to another company." (See Strategy 13—Using Another Offer Even When You Don't Have One.) If a headhunter is involved, you can contact the recruiter to find out what the company is thinking. (See Strategy 19—Using the Headhunter to Help You Negotiate.) However you determine to respond, as long as you understand that the delay may be a tactic to try to pressure you into conceding on a key point, you will not let it affect the way you bargain. Moreover, sometimes a delay in getting back to you may not be a tactic at all. Rather, the negotiator may have a legitimate reason for not calling, such as the need to get approval from someone who is unavailable.

It is important to understand the effect silence can have on the person you are bargaining with, and on you if you allow it to. As a rule, you want to control the pace of the negotiations and the agenda. Using silence to your advantage is one way to do that. Be careful, however, not to overuse this technique. Neither silence nor delay should be used to such an extent that the company thinks you are unreliable or you don't care about the job. After all, your reliability and enthusiasm are part of the reason you were offered the job in the first place.

Summary of Negotiating Points

- Use silence as a negotiating tool.
- When you have made your point, remain silent until the other side responds.
- Often it is best to let the other side make the next move; silence will encourage them to do so.
- When you are not sure what to do or when things are not going the way you want, find a reason to take a break.
- A well-timed delay in getting back to the company can work to your advantage.
- Do not let the company negotiator use silence or delay to pressure you.
- Be careful not to use silence or delay to such an extent that the company thinks you are unreliable or don't care about the job.

24

How to Win by Conceding

There are occasions where it us undoubtedly
better to incur loss than to make gain.
TITUS MACCIUS PLAUTUS

In labor negotiations, it is considered bargaining in bad faith not to offer concessions. This method of negotiating is referred to as "Boulwarism," after one of the more famous practitioners of this approach. Boulware was a vice president of labor relations at General Electric in the 1950s who believed that the way to negotiate with a union was to start out with a reasonable proposal and steadfastly refuse to change your position. The National Labor Relations Board, the government agency responsible for regulating labor relations, ruled that negotiating in this manner constituted illegal bad-faith bargaining. Failing to offer concessions, according to the National Labor Relations Board, was the equivalent of not bargaining at all. Even when this technique is successful, it leaves the other side feeling taken advantage of. As a result, in most types of negotiating, the practice is frowned upon. This is particularly important in employment negotiations, where how you handle yourself while bargaining will provide the basis for your new employer's first impression of you.

Giving in Order to Get

Our commonly shared understanding of fairness calls for a reciprocating gesture when someone has given us something. Cultural norms dictate that when one side makes a concession during negotiations, the other side respond in kind. This is part of the etiquette of negotiating. When bargaining about the terms of your employment, you ought to take advantage of it.

The obvious conclusion here is that the best way to gain a concession is to give one. It is important tactically to ask for concessions immediately after you have agreed to something. When it comes to negotiating, people have very short memories.

At the beginning of the negotiations, try to determine how the company responds to concessions. When you raise a concern, does the negotiator react without the need to bargain (the "problem solver")? Or does the negotiator consider conceding too easily to be a sign of weakness (the "macho negotiator")? Is it sufficient to concede on a point and then follow up by asking for a concession later (the "fair trader")? Or is it necessary to make the *quid pro quo* explicit (the "horse trader")? When a horse trader asks you for a concession, you will need to condition your agreement on the company's consenting to one or more of your requests. Thus, instead of simply offering to forget about the no-interest home loan you had asked for and hoping that the company negotiator will respond favorably, you need to request something specific in return. For example, you might indicate that if the company was willing to give you a signing bonus, it could avoid the problem it seemed to be having with your request for a no-interest home loan. Unfortunately, most negotiators do not fall neatly into one category or another. Their response will vary depending on the issue. You should do the same. It is usually best at first to try a problem-solving approach. If that doesn't work, use the horse trader approach for major concessions and a fair trader approach for minor ones.

Concessions can be used when the negotiations start to bog down or when you reach an impasse on a particular issue. Do not make a concession too readily, even if it is unimportant to you. The company negotiator will not value what you are giving up if you do not act as if it is meaningful. Ordinarily, you should make only one concession at a time. Also, be able to provide plausible-sounding justifications for changes in your negotiating position. Explanations can be based on your attempts to accommodate the company's needs, concessions granted by the company, new information, or changes in your circumstances. Properly timed concessions will allow you to appear cooperative and should get the negotiations moving again on a positive note. The strategic use of concessions throughout the negotiations can help you achieve the objectives that are most important to you.

Use the early stages of the negotiations to explore the company's position on the issues. Go over each aspect of the offer. Clarify anything you don't understand. Ask questions about why certain aspects of the proposals, such as bonus criteria, are structured the way they are. Determine if there is flexibility on various items. In response to any proposal that appears to be unusual, question whether the company has experienced problems in the past that have resulted in the need for such a proposal. Gather as much information as possible. (See Strategy 3—Seek and You Shall Find: The Tactical Use of Questions.)

Try to determine why the company negotiator is taking a certain stance. The negotiator may provide a good reason to justify the position being taken or may simply fall back on company policy. Sometimes you will not be given any reason at all. It is possible that the negotiator simply does not have the authority to agree and may not want to go back to the company to get it. [See Strategy 21—Bypass the Negotiator (Unless It's Your Future Boss).] One of your objectives during these early discussions is to determine what issues are important to the company and where it has bargaining flexibility. Depending on the nature of the negotiations and the level of the executive involved, this part of the process may last less than an hour or can extend over several days. It is also a good idea, after an initial session in which you have asked a lot of questions, to request a little time to digest the information you have received.

Timing Your Concessions

It is best not to concede issues too early during the preliminary discussions. Thoroughly discussing issues will enable you to identify those areas where the company is either not willing or not able to give in. Typically a company will turn down a seemingly reasonable request because of concern with the impact that granting it might have on the organization. A prospective employer might willingly agree to something if you were the only person affected, but it is not likely to disrupt the whole organization just to hire you. If, for example, a company provides all its sales representatives with midsize American cars, it is not going to agree to your request for a BMW, even if you would be willing to accept a lower salary in return. To do so would result in other sales representatives asking for BMWs. The fact that the company was able to negotiate a lower salary as a result will be lost on your peers. Similarly, a company will ordinarily not risk upsetting its salary structure by paying you substantially more than others at your level.

Concessions can be effectively used to conclude the negotiations. If you have identified the right issue on which to concede, offering it as part of a package to resolve all the outstanding issues will maximize the impact of that concession and enable you to reach agreement. This technique is frequently used by car dealers. At the point where you have almost reached agreement on the price of the car, the salesperson says: "That is the best I can do on the price, but if we can reach an agreement today I'll throw in the gold package at no extra charge." By this time, the salesperson has gotten you to the point where you see yourself driving along the highway in that new red convertible. Now, with the chance to get the gold package for free, the deal is too good to pass up. Of course, in agreeing to the dealer's offer you are giving up the possibility of getting any further price reduction. The desire to complete the deal coupled with the last-minute offer of the gold package is too much to resist. (See Strategy 8—Creating a Stake in the Outcome.) That is why using a concession to close the deal is so powerful.

In employment negotiations, this technique works basically the same way. After you have thoroughly explored the company's position, you can begin to lay the groundwork. By this time you should have identified one or more issues that are important to the company. You will want to get as much as possible in return for agreeing to the company's position on these issues. To do that, you need to understand that some of the issues are essentially nonnegotiable. The reason, as discussed previously, is that agreeing to them would affect the rest of the organization. When you discuss these points during the negotiations, provide the employer with all the reasons that it should agree to your request. Be forceful in your arguments. Don't let the company negotiator pressure you into agreeing before you are ready.

Generally there will be a number of areas in the employer's initial offer that you will want to change. Some of them will be important to the company; others won't. Part of the process is to determine where there is room for give-and-take. As the discussions proceed, you will need to yield on some issues in return for other concessions. To be able to use a concession to close the deal, however, you must unyieldingly maintain your position on at least one issue of importance to the employer until the very end.

Once you get to the point where you have agreed on almost everything, you are ready to make the most of your final concession. Of the issues that remain, at least one must be an issue that is important to the company. The more important the company negotiator believes this issue is to you, the more valuable it will be when you concede it. The other outstanding issues should be limited to one or two things that you want but have not yet been able to get the company to agree to. The magnitude of what you are seeking should be approximately equal to, or preferably less than, that of the concession you are about to make.

Offer to concede on the remaining key issue of concern to the company in order to reach a final agreement. In return, ask the company to acquiesce on the other outstanding issues. If more than one or two requests are still on the table or if other nonnegotiable issues remain, you will need to drop them as well. Provided that you have properly judged the importance of the issue you are conceding, the company will likely agree to accept your position on the other issues in order to reach agreement.

Concluding the Negotiations

Let's look at how this works in a concrete situation. Assume you are a job candidate for the technology company, described earlier, that requires all its employees to sign a standard agreement not to compete. Early on you identify the agreement as an issue which is not negotiable. Everyone without exception is required to sign it. You ask to limit the number of companies to which the noncompete restrictions would apply. The negotiator tells you the company cannot do that. You ask to reduce the period covered by the restrictions from two years to one year. The company denies that request as well. Then you move on to discuss other issues. At this point most of the outstanding items are resolved. The only issue that remains—other than the agreement not to compete—is severance. Now is the time to offer a concession to get the company to agree to what you want.

The conclusion of the negotiations might go something like this:

> YOU: I understand that the agreement not to compete that you want me to sign is very important to the company. It creates a lot of problems for me, though. But if you can't change it, I guess I'll agree to sign it in order to get this thing wrapped up.
>
> NEGOTIATOR: That's good.
>
> YOU: Since that noncompete will probably keep me from working, I'm sure you will agree to a one-year severance package.
>
> NEGOTIATOR: I don't know.
>
> YOU: I really could not possibly agree to the noncompete unless I had the security of a reasonable severance package in case things didn't work out.
>
> NEGOTIATOR: One year is a very large severance package.
>
> YOU: Then why don't we make the noncompete for six months?
>
> NEGOTIATOR: OK, we have a deal.

It is important not to appear to be manipulative when you use concessions. No one wants to feel taken advantage of. To avoid giving that appearance, select an issue about which you have legitimate concerns. If an issue is of critical importance to the company, it most likely involves you giving up something of real value. Properly done, the use of a concession to conclude the negotiations allows you to maximize what you get in return.

When you are granting concessions, trust your instincts. Generally it is a good idea to vary your approach. Sometimes you can simply concede on a point and follow up with a request for something else. At other times you will want to offer to trade one item directly for another. ("I'll forget about anything over and above the company's regular relocation policy if you'll give me a signing bonus which I can use to cover any additional moving expenses.") Occasionally you may concede without asking for anything in return simply to gain some goodwill. Remember, however, that your goal is not to win the congeniality award. It is to get the best possible deal.

Always try to keep something in reserve in order to wrap up the negotiations. It might be something that you want but know the company is not willing to agree to, or it might be something that the company needs you to agree to. It could be something important to you which you are willing to give up if the overall package is sufficiently attractive. On the other hand, it could be an issue that is actually less important to you than you have let on. (See Strategy 15—Creating Red Herring Issues.) Whatever issue you select, wait until the time is right and use it to reach a final agreement.

Throughout the negotiations, granting concessions strategically will enable you to get a better deal. As the process nears a conclusion, concessions can be used to maximum effect. Making a concession at the end of the negotiations may enable you to obtain something you could not have gotten the company to agree to at an earlier stage. This is, in part, because by this time the company already has a major stake in ensuring a successful outcome. (See Strategy 8—Creating a Stake in the Outcome.) It is also effective because it allows the company negotiator to feel like a winner. (See Strategy 20—Making the Company Negotiator Look Good.)

Summary of Negotiating Points

- Don't concede on issues too early.
- Thoroughly discuss the company's initial offer before you begin negotiating.

- Identify issues that are of critical importance to the company.
- Agree to concessions strategically and vary your approach.
- Generally follow a concession immediately with a request to reciprocate.
- Always try to keep in reserve an issue that is important to the company to use to close the deal.

25
Walking Away

He has departed, withdrawn, gone away.
CICERO

Of all the negotiations I have been involved in, the one that I am most proud of is one that did not end with my client accepting the job—at least not the job for which we were initially negotiating. My client was the president of a midsize company. He had been approached about joining its main competitor as president. The compensation package he was offered was significantly more than he was earning, including a substantial amount of stock. With a little effort we were even able to get the company to improve the financial terms of the deal.

The only problem we encountered was getting a satisfactory severance package if things didn't work out. Although severance is always important, I felt that in his case it was critical. The prospective employer was not doing well, and it was rumored that the parent company might sell it off. We asked for a severance of 18 months' salary and benefits continuation, extended to two years' severance in the event of a change of control (i.e., a sale of the business). Equally important to my client was that the vesting of the restricted stock and stock options he was to be given be accelerated in the event he lost his job.

Despite our best effort, we were not able to get the company to agree to an acceptable severance package. In light of the company's situation, I counseled my client not to accept the job without a suitable severance package. Although I thought we might eventually reach a satisfactory resolution of the severance issue, my client decided he did not want to work for this company. He reasoned: "If it's this hard to get agreement on a reasonable severance package, what's it going to be like actually working for this company?" So he walked away from the deal.

The story does not end there. We decided to use the offer to see if we could get his current employer to improve his current compensation and to give him some assurances about being promoted to chief executive officer in the near future. To avoid the risk that he would be considered disloyal, we decided not to use the offer to get his current employer to bid against it. (See Strategy 13—Using Another Offer Even When You Don't Have One.) The executive told his boss about the offer and made it clear that he was not going to accept it. He explained why he had considered the offer. He asked for help in resolving his concerns because he really wanted to stay with the current employer.

As it turned out, walking away was the right decision. My client was given a substantial raise, additional stock, and a promise that he would be considered for the chief executive job in the next two years. He is now chairman of the company. As for the company that tried to recruit him, it was sold to another company within six months and its chief executive officer lost his job, presumably without the benefit of an adequate severance package.

The best way to ensure that you get a good deal is to be able to walk away. To do that, it helps if you are satisfied remaining in your current position or have more than one other job possibility in the works at any given time. When you are not desperate to take a job, you will bargain with more confidence knowing it will not be the end of the world if this particular deal does not go through. You will also be able to ask for more when you are not afraid of losing this particular opportunity. This is not a strategy; it is a philosophy which applies to every negotiation. It is also essential when you employ a "walking away" strategy. By definition, this is a high-risk stratagem. As the name implies, there is always the possibility that you are saying good-by to the job. When you adopt a walking-away strategy, you have to be prepared for that possibility. And, of course, not taking a particular job sometimes can be the best thing you can do. You will find that out, however, only in hindsight after you have obtained a better job with a better compensation package elsewhere. At other times just showing that you are willing to walk away will greatly strengthen your bargaining position.

This is such a risky strategy that you need to be careful in determining when to use it. One of those times is when you are certain that there is no way you would accept the job unless the employer changes its bargaining position. In that case, you have nothing to lose by employing a walking-away strategy. Another time is when the prospective employer really needs or wants to hire you. Be careful, however, because rarely do employers ever need or want employees so desperately. If you are relying on the employer crumbling at the very thought of not being able to hire you, you are very likely to be disappointed

Your goal is to walk away from the negotiations without foreclosing the possibility that the company will reconsider its position and make you a substantially better offer. How you do that is the key to using a walking-away strategy. When you are implementing this strategy, you need to be gracious to the negotiator. Compliment the negotiator on how the negotiations were handled. Extend your thanks for all the negotiator's efforts. Try to place the blame for the failure of the negotiations on some objective impediment to reaching agreement. Employing traditional negotiating theory, you might describe the situation as one where the circles simply do not overlap. (See Strategy 5—Creating a Win-Win Situation.) While expressing your regrets about not being able to accept the offer, remind the company negotiator of all the reasons you were excited about the job in the first place. Finally, let the negotiator know that if another position becomes available for which the company could satisfy your salary requirements or overcome whatever the stumbling block is, you would be interested in being considered.

By so doing, you are letting the negotiator know that the reason you are turning down the offer has nothing to do with the job or the company or the way the negotiator handled the process. If you were declining the offer for any one of those reasons, there would be no room for the company to come back to you with a new proposal. By focusing on objective impediments to the deal, you make it clear that if the company can figure out a way to remove the obstacles you would be happy to take the job. As a result, the negotiator is not boxed into a corner and forced to try to justify how the negotiations were handled. If the negotiator's position on the thorny issues does not really constitute the company's bottom line, then a compromise should be reachable. If there are real obstacles to reaching an agreement, you have given the negotiator the opportunity to become a hero by figuring out how to overcome them. In any event, you have left the door open to further negotiations.

Let's assume you are ready to walk away from a job offer over the issue of stock options. You have asked for a grant of a certain number of stock options immediately and additional options a year from now if you meet certain prescribed criteria. The company does not want to give you any stock options until you have been on board a year and have proved yourself. It also wants any award of stock options to be discretionary. The company negotiator appears to be unwilling to agree to specific criteria for the award of those options. You like the company and are excited about the job it is offering you. However, without a guarantee of sufficient equity in the company, it does not make financial sense for you to accept the job. How do you walk away and still leave the door open for further negotiations? Your conversation might go something like this:

YOU: Unfortunately, it doesn't look like this is going to work.

NEGOTIATOR: What do you mean?

YOU: I am really excited about the job, but there is no way I could take it without getting a significant amount of equity. I would be giving up too much. I really appreciate your effort to put this deal together. It's too bad the company couldn't figure out a way to give me more stock.

NEGOTIATOR: I don't know if I can do anything, but let me talk to my boss again.

One twist to this approach is to let the company negotiator know that you intend to drop a note to the hiring manager (assuming that manager is not the one negotiating with you) simply to say what a fine job the negotiator did and how sorry you are that you could not accept the offer because of whatever it was that the company could not agree to. The possibility that you might write such a letter is likely to cause a negotiator who has room to improve an offer a great deal of discomfort. A person in that position might improve the offer simply to avoid being second-guessed as to why improvements weren't made in the first place.

When you employ a walking-away strategy, you need to be prepared for the fact that the company may not make you another offer. As long as you are willing to walk away from the job, however, and don't close the door to further negotiations, you have accomplished your goals. You have strengthened your bargaining position by making it clear that you won't accept the job unless the company can satisfy your needs. More important, you have not forced the company into a corner by presenting an ultimatum. You have, regretfully, had to withdraw your candidacy and you have done so in a way that indicates your motive has nothing to do with the company, the job, or the negotiator. Such an approach gives the negotiator a chance to solve the problems standing in the way of your accepting the job.

Summary of Negotiating Points

- Be prepared psychologically to walk away from an offer.
- Try to have more than one job possibility in the works.
- Do not accept a position unless it meets your minimum criteria.
- Never frame requests as ultimatums.
- Explain your problems with the offer.
- Reiterate all the reasons you would have liked to accept the job.
- Extend your thanks for the negotiator's efforts.
- Leave the door open to further negotiations.

Job Security: How to Ensure That You Get to Enjoy the Fruits of Your Negotiations

An oral contract is as good as the paper it is written on.   ANONYMOUS

After she was fired from her job Janet received her severance package, but the company refused to pay her the annual bonus she thought she had been guaranteed. She showed me her offer letter, which stated that she was guaranteed a bonus of at least $20,000. It was unclear from the letter how long the guarantee was to last, although Janet clearly understood at the time she was hired that a portion of her bonus was to be guaranteed each year. Unfortunately, the person who hired her, and who sent her the letter, was no longer with the company. As a result, the company chose to interpret the guarantee language as covering only the first year of employment. Even though I thought Janet might prevail in court, we discussed the costs and the risks involved. I suggested that it would be difficult for her to find a new job if potential employers found out she was suing her previous employer.

When Janet informed higher-ups at the company that her attorney thought she was entitled to the bonus, they made it clear that, if they were sued, they would not do business with her in the future. Because she was considering becoming a consultant, she had to take that threat seriously. Despite her appeals to fairness, the company refused to concede on this issue. Janet decided not to sue.

Get It in Writing

Because of greater executive mobility today, as well as the large number of mergers, acquisitions, and downsizings, even executives who are performing well are likely to lose their jobs at some time during their career. When people change jobs, there are frequently mismatches in terms of personality, corporate culture, and job fit. As a result, issues surrounding termination have become more important today than ever before.

It will do you little good to have obtained, through your negotiating efforts, an excellent salary, generous stock options, lots of perks, and the job of your dreams if you can be summarily dismissed without a sufficient severance package. If you fail to satisfactorily negotiate the terms under which you can be terminated, you risk losing everything else you may have achieved.

While you are being recruited, the person seeking to hire you will likely make all sorts of promises and representations concerning job security. However, when you are being terminated, the company will ordinarily disregard any promises you thought had been made to you, particularly if the person making them is no longer there. Instead, it will be guided by its regular severance policy, unless you have a written agreement clearly requiring that you be afforded a better severance package.

Even though verbal promises, if you can prove that they were made, are enforceable in a court of law, more often than not it does not make sense to sue your former employer. Therefore, to protect what you worked so hard to achieve through the negotiating process, you need to have the terms of employment spelled out in writing. This does not have to be a 20-page formal contract drafted by your lawyer. It can be a simple confirmation letter signed by a representative of the company clearly setting forth the basic terms that have been agreed to. Not only is such a letter legally enforceable, but if the terms are plainly spelled out it is much less likely that a lawsuit will ever be necessary.

Even if you do not get everything you want, whatever you do get you can certainly get in writing. At a minimum, the two key issues that should be covered in that agreement are compensation and termination. For the reasons discussed above, termination is probably the more critical issue. Other important issues that should be covered are the job description, the company's right to transfer you, your reporting relationship, vesting of stock and options, perks, benefits, and what happens in the event of death or disability.

If things go well, you will not need any form of agreement. Your employer will be happy with you and will want to make you happy. However, if things don't go as planned, if there is a takeover, if you get a new boss, or if there is just not a good fit, then you are going to wish you had spelled out what had been agreed upon in writing; and as odd as this may sound, so will the company. In light of the increased likelihood of employment litigation, companies are more likely to want to enter into an agreement at the outset of the employment relationship which spells out under what circumstances you can be terminated and what you get in the event that occurs.

First you need to determine whether the company routinely provides new hires with employment contracts and, if so, at what levels. (See Getting Ready to Negotiate.) If you happen to be at a level where contracts are routinely offered, then getting an employment contract won't be an issue. In most cases you will not be at that level. If you are not, you will probably want to use a "confirmation letter" to spell out the terms you have agreed to accept, rather than seek a formal employment contract. If they are approached correctly, companies will rarely refuse to put in writing what has been agreed upon. Even companies that, as a matter of policy, do not offer "employment contracts," usually send new hires "offer letters" setting forth the terms of employment. Those letters, if properly written, will serve the same purpose as an employment contract and will most likely be enforceable in a court of law. You can send a confirmation letter which will not only serve the same purpose but will allow you to determine how the agreed-upon terms are described. The difference between a confirmation letter and an offer letter is that the former is written by you and signed by the company, whereas the latter is sent to you by the company.

Once you have determined that you are not going to seek a formal employment contract, how should you go about getting what has been agreed to in writing? At the conclusion of the negotiations you might simply state that you "will confirm the terms that have been agreed upon in a letter just to make sure there are no misunderstandings." Particularly if you have been using memos throughout the negotiations, this suggestion will seem routine and is not likely to engender any opposition. (See Strategy 7—Using the Follow-up Memo as a Negotiating Tool.) The language that you have agreed upon by memo during the negotiations should be incorporated into the final confirmation letter. At the end of that letter, either you can request the employer to sign indicating that the letter accurately reflects the terms of the job offer or you can ask the employer to incorporate those terms into an offer letter.

On occasion, the person you are dealing with might respond to your suggestion of sending a confirmation letter with "What do you need a letter for? Don't you trust me?" If you are negotiating with your future boss such a reaction is especially problematic. If that occurs, you need to depersonalize the situation and respond along the following lines: "This has nothing to do with you individually. In fact, if I was certain that you would always be here, I would be perfectly happy just to rely on your word. However, tomorrow you might get hit by a bus or leave the company. I think it would be helpful, in order to avoid any possible misunderstandings, if we put down in writing what has been agreed upon."

Termination

You must resolve two basic questions about termination when you negotiate the terms of your employment: (1) Under what circumstances can you be terminated? and (2) What will you receive if you are terminated? Many employers have policies which state that they are "employers at will." An "at will" employer can fire an employee for any reason or no reason. Sometimes employers will specifically include "at will" language in their offer letters. More often, if nothing is agreed to about the employer's right to terminate you, the company will state in its offer letter that you are being hired "subject to all the company's policies." If that is all that is said, you are likely to be an "at will" employee, because the company probably has a policy saying that all employees, unless otherwise specifically agreed, are "at will." Of course, if at all possible, you do not want to agree to be an "at will" employee.

As an employee, you would like to get your employer to guarantee your employment for a certain term or else limit the right to terminate you to instances of serious misconduct. Most employment arrangements which are not "at will," even those for a specified term, provide that an employee can be terminated "for cause" or "for good cause." In addition, they typically allow for termination "without cause" if the company makes certain specified payments and provides certain benefits. Therefore what is typically at stake in the determination of whether a discharge is "for cause" is your right to receive severance, bonuses, benefits continuation, outplacement, and/or accelerated vesting of your stock or options.

Employers today are insisting that most employees below a certain level be treated as "employees at will." If you are being hired by such an employer, instead of trying to limit the company's termination rights, you can achieve the same results simply by getting the company to agree to pay severance in the event you are terminated "without cause." As part of that severance package you can include payment of current-year bonuses, benefits continuation, outplacement, and/or accelerated vesting of your stock or options. Strategically the issue of severance should be depersonalized and dealt with as an issue that needs to be covered in the event that the person you are dealing with leaves the company, just as you approached the overall need to have your terms of employment spelled out in writing.

If you have a strong bargaining position, you may want to include a definition of "cause," which you will want to define narrowly, spelling out the types of conduct which will constitute "cause." Otherwise, as is more typically the case, it is generally best simply to state that the company can "terminate you for cause." Strategically, if you are seeking to get the company's agreement to include a termination for cause provision as part of their offer, it is a good idea to emphasize that you are not seeking to prevent the employer from firing you if it is unhappy with your performance. Rather, you are merely trying to ensure that you are provided a sufficient severance to allow you to take care of your family (if you are not married you can substitute your "aged mother," "yourself," "your dog," or "your foster child in Guatemala") until you find another job. In that context it is only fair that you be paid severance unless your termination is for cause.

You may also want to get your employer's agreement to provide you with written notice of any performance problems and a reasonable opportunity to correct them before you can be fired, or at least, provide written notice of the specific reasons for termination if you are fired. When an employer is required to articulate in writing the reasons for discharge, that requirement in and of itself serves as a check against arbitrary terminations. Your employer will think carefully before terminating you for a reason which, once spelled out in writing, may have to be defended in court.

After an agreement is reached on when you can be terminated, you need to determine what you will get in that event. How much severance you will be entitled to is usually the first issue that must be resolved. Most severance policies are based on length of service. The longer you work for the company, the more you are paid in severance. Anywhere from one week per year to one month per year of service is typical. However, since you are most at risk of losing your job in the first year of employment, it is important to seek a minimum amount of severance regardless of your length of service. You could expect to get anywhere from two weeks to one year as a minimum severance, depending on the level of your position and the industry you are in.

Once you have agreed upon the amount of severance, the company may raise other issues such as whether the severance will be paid as salary continuation (most executives want it paid as a lump sum) and whether earnings from other employment will be used to offset the company's severance obligations. Often companies will raise these conditions for payment of severance only after the amount of severance has been agreed upon, stating that is how severance is paid. You can preempt this negotiating tactic by framing your initial request for severance to be paid as a lump sum upon termination. Whether you agree to accept payment of severance as salary continuation or to allow earnings from other employment to be used to offset the company's severance obligations will depend on your bargaining position, company practices (see Strategy 18—Looking for Exceptions), and the total amount of severance being offered (see Strategy 10—Be Flexible: Consider the Possibilities).

When negotiating severance, don't forget to ask for continuation of your benefits as well. Although companies are required by law to offer you the option of continuing your heath benefits at your expense, you ought to be seeking to continue all your benefits at company expense, as if you remained employed. Medical benefits in particular are expensive. Moreover, when you are hired, most companies will readily include the continuation of those benefits at company expense as part of a negotiated severance arrangement. Since the severance period is usually determined by the amount of time it should reasonably take someone at that level to find another job, you can persuasively argue that benefits should be continued for an equivalent period of time. Most companies will, in fact, agree to continue benefits following a termination "without cause" for a period of time equal to the severance period.

The other major termination issues that you need to concern yourself with are how your bonus and any unvested stock or options will be treated. In the event you are terminated without cause, your employer will ordinarily not pay you any bonuses unless the criteria for receiving them have already been fully achieved. You may, however, be able to get the company to agree to pay you a prorated portion of your targeted bonus, or the guaranteed portion of that bonus if there is any. With regard to stock or options, companies will sometimes agree to allow vesting on a prorated basis or even allow the stock or options to continue to vest during the severance period. For purposes of negotiating, you have a powerful argument as to why you should receive such benefits. After all, these are benefits that are being offered to entice you to leave your current place of employment, where you are probably receiving similar benefits. All you are asking is that they be given to you in the event that you are terminated without cause.

Diminution of Responsibilities and Transfers

Once you have dealt with the issues governing termination, you need to protect yourself against certain methods that unethical companies use to try to circumvent the protections you have negotiated. Even if the company you are joining has an excellent reputation, it may be taken over by someone else and you may need these protections. For instance, it is important to make certain that your duties and title are clearly spelled out in your offer letter and that they cannot be changed without your agreement. Although your future employer will want some flexibility to change job responsibilities to meet changing needs, most companies will agree to include language such as the following:

> The company will employ you as vice president of marketing, with such duties, responsibilities, and authority as are consistent with that position.

This type of language in an offer letter will prevent an employer from trying to force you to leave the company without having to fire you in order to avoid paying severance or other termination benefits. Also, executives who leave a company on their own are prevented from arguing that agreements not to compete should not be enforced because they were terminated without cause.

For example, if you have not spelled out in your confirmation letter what your job duties are, you can simply be assigned tasks which you find unacceptable or which might hurt your marketability, in an effort to get you to resign. Although an employer is generally required to act in good faith, it is also free, in the absence of an agreement to the contrary, to assign an employee different job duties. Therefore, if you have not protected yourself and the company is not too blatant in its efforts to force you out (e.g., by assigning a vice president of marketing to run the warehouse), you may have to suffer those new responsibilities or forfeit your severance.

You may also want to spell out your reporting relationship. Even though you have defined your job duties, companies can effectively diminish your status by making you report to someone at your level or, depending on how those duties are defined, by removing your operating responsibilities and assigning you to "special projects". If you do not protect yourself, you will leave yourself open to efforts by an unscrupulous company to force you to resign and thereby deprive you of the severance benefits you negotiated.

Similarly, you need to protect yourself against being transferred without your consent. You might do this, for example, by having your offer letter state: "You will be based in New York City or within a reasonable commute from there (not to exceed 30 miles), unless you agree otherwise." This gives the company reasonable flexibility to move its offices but at the same time prevents the company from forcing you to move in order to keep your job. It also protects you against an unscrupulous employer that would use the threat of a transfer to force you to resign without having to pay you severance or other termination benefits. Unless you are fond of the idea of heading the company's new Anchorage, Alaska facility, you will be glad that you restricted the company's ability to transfer you without your consent. You cannot prevent the company from transferring your job responsibilities to another location for a legitimate business reason. You can, however, ensure that you have the option of moving to that new location or receiving the severance and other termination benefits you are entitled to if you elect not to do so.

Death or Disability

You also need to cover what happens in the event of your death or disability. Companies generally offer their executives long-term disability insurance, usually with the employees paying the premium. Most long-term disability plans, however, require that disabled employees be out of work for a specified time period, ordinarily six months, before becoming eligible to receive disability benefits. Therefore, you will want to get your prospective employer to agree to continue to pay your salary in the event you are unable to work because of a disability until you are eligible to begin receiving long-term disability benefits.

Typically a company will not agree to pay you severance benefits in the event of your death or a termination due to disability, because presumably that has been covered through the life and long-term disability insurance provided by the employer. You still need to deal with the issue of bonuses and the vesting of stock and options in the event of termination due to death or disability. You might seek the full value of any bonuses that would have been earned during the final year of your employment and the vesting of all unvested stock or options in the event of your death or disability termination. An employer, however, is more likely to agree to provide those benefits on a pro rata basis. You should also carefully review the applicable option and bonus plans before spending time and effort, and negotiating capital, on these issues. Ordinarily stock and stock option plans, but not bonus plans, deal with what happens in the event of death or disability. You may also want to have your employer continue providing benefits to your surviving dependents for a period of time after your death.

Agreements Not to Compete

Employers today often ask their employees to sign agreements not to compete. These agreements generally provide that, while the employee works for the company and for one or two years after the termination of employment, the employee will not go to work for a competitor. You should be very careful about agreeing to such terms. Although there are limits on the enforceability of covenants not to compete, if they are reasonable, in most states they are enforceable. Moreover, when you enter into an agreement not to compete, it may keep you from getting a job in the industry that you know best. Before you accept an offer of employment you should ask if you will have to sign an agreement not to compete and, if so, request to see it.

Many employees do not worry about an agreement not to compete because they believe either that it won't be enforceable or that the company won't choose to enforce it. Notwithstanding, you should never sign anything that you would not want to be bound by on the hopes that it won't be enforced. Even if an agreement not to compete is unenforceable, a company interested in hiring you may be reluctant to do so if it means that a lawsuit goes along with it. In addition, employers sometimes link agreements not to compete to the payout of severance and bonuses or the vesting of stock and options as a means of enforcing them without going to court. If you violate such an agreement, the company will not pay your severance and/or bonuses. Supplemental pensions are also sometimes conditioned on complying with noncompete agreements.

If you have to enter into an agreement not to compete, make sure that it is drawn narrowly. For example, instead of simply agreeing not to go to work for "a competitor," get the company to define what it considers to be areas of competition. Better still, get your future employer to list the companies it does not want you to work for when you leave. Limit, as much as possible, the length of time the agreement will be in force as well as the geographic scope of the agreement. Seek legal advice if you are asked to sign an agreement not to compete.

Another restriction employers often seek is an agreement not to disclose trade secrets or confidential information that is provided to employees during the course of their employment. In addition, if you are in a creative field, a prospective employer will want the rights to any inventions or discoveries you make during the term of your employment. Finally, you may be asked to agree not to hire or solicit company employees once you leave the company. With any of these types of agreements, it is important to narrowly define what it is you are agreeing to and to protect your freedom of movement to the greatest extent possible. It is also important to seek appropriate legal advice. Although you may have to agree to some restrictions on your postemployment activity, in return you ought to be able to improve your severance package by arguing that those restrictions will make it more difficult to find another job.

Summary of Key Points

- Have the terms that are agreed upon spelled out in writing and signed by someone on behalf of the company.

- Be certain to cover the issues of when you can be terminated and what you will receive in the event you are terminated.

- Determine if employment contracts are generally given to employees at your level.

- If not, use a confirmation or offer letter to spell out, in writing, what has been agreed upon.

- If it becomes a major issue, depersonalize your reason for wanting a written confirmation of the offer terms.

- Protect yourself against attempts to force you to resign in order to avoid paying you severance.

- If you have to enter into an agreement not to compete, negotiate the terms narrowly.

- Don't sign an agreement you would not want to be bound by in the belief that it is not enforceable or is not likely to be enforced.

- Seek legal advice where appropriate.

Gender Differences in Employment Negotiations

*They are convinced that its success with some
women means it will work with all women.
No amount of saying that we, like men, are a
segmented market, that we don't all think
alike, does any good.*

GLORIA STEINEM (ON A CIGARETTE MAKER'S
ADVERTISING CAMPAIGN)

If you are a woman reading this chapter, you are probably asking yourself, "Why should I listen to a man give advice about how women should
negotiate? My sister, a successful sales executive, asked me the same
question. Then she went on to remind me of an old joke, the punchline of
which is that most men don't understand women, and the few that do are
always exhausted." Although I don't purport to "understand women," I
have had the opportunity to observe women who are effective as negotiators and women who are not. I have advised women in negotiating
their employment agreements; I have hired women and had to negotiate
with them; and I have worked with women who are excellent negotiators.

Before writing this chapter, I discussed the topic with successful busi-
nesswomen, executive recruiters specializing in the placement of women,
and career coaches who have worked extensively with women execu-

tives. One thing they all agree on is that the dynamics of negotiating are different when women negotiate with men, and even when women negotiate with other women, than when men negotiate with men. Maxine Hartley, an executive recruiter who heads the diversity practice at Pearl Management L.L.C., summed it up nicely: "Men and women are different and they negotiate differently." Women who understand those differences are likely to be more successful when they negotiate the terms of their employment.

One female labor negotiator I know well has been very effective by being "one of the guys." She is loud. She can drink and swear with the best of them. Although on occasion she uses the fact that she is an attractive woman to her advantage, her negotiating style can be best described as " persistent and tough." She wears her opponents down. Most women and a lot of men could not successfully use this negotiating style. She tempers this aggressive style with a good sense of humor and makes it work for her, not only when she negotiates with unions but in employment negotiations as well.

A good starting point for developing a successful negotiating style is to be yourself. Some women, like my friend, can be successful with a negotiating style similar to the "aggressive" style favored by many men. However, women should not necessarily mimic the negotiating styles that have been successful for men; rather, they should take advantage of the style that works best for them. Since a confrontational style usually is not the best approach to take in employment negotiations even for men, women are generally well advised to adopt a more cooperative negotiating style. (See Strategy 5—Creating a Win-Win Situation.) At the same time, women need to be firm in their resolve to achieve the objectives they set for themselves. The best negotiators, men or women, don't allow their ego to get in the way of their strategy. Some of the most successful women negotiators take advantage of the competitiveness many men bring to negotiations and not only defuse it but use it against them.

When women negotiate, they tend not to go directly to the topic they want to discuss. They circle more and take longer to get to where they want to go. In so doing, they often make good use of questions. (See Strategy 3—Seek and You Shall Find: The Tactical Use of Questions.) Men, on the other hand, try to build credibility and then go in for the kill. They are also generally better able to remain emotionally detached from the process. Women frequently forget that disagreements during negotiations are not personal. (See Strategy 9—Disagree Without Being Disagreeable: Being Likable as a Negotiating Strategy.)

Each of the strategies set forth in this book can be used just as effectively by women as by men. Since all women are not alike, these strategies need to be adjusted to suit each individual's negotiating style.

There is no one right way for women to negotiate. This chapter is intended to help you avoid the most common mistakes women make during employment negotiations.

The biggest mistake women make is to ask for too little. This is a common problem for men as well. (See Strategy 2—Asking for More: You Can't Get It If You Don't Ask.) However, women tend almost uniformly to underestimate their worth. If men generally should ask for 10 percent more than they think they are worth, women should ask for 25 percent more. Vivian Eyre, a New York career consultant who is president of Partners for Women's Growth Inc., describes how women typically visualize a negotiation in their head beforehand and anticipate a negative response. As a result, they ask for too little or don't ask for certain things at all.

Vivian also describes a problem which holds back many women when they negotiate. She calls the phenomenon being "rules-oriented." Vivian illustrated it with the following story about one of her clients. Suzanne had been hired by a publishing company to head a new publishing imprint. She agreed to accept a higher base salary with a lower bonus because she was told that the company's compensation policy was to provide a greater portion of compensation in base salary and less in bonus. Through her talent and hard work, Suzanne was able to increase revenues in her first year by more than 30 percent. She was recognized for her accomplishments by her peers and her boss. However, the closer she got to the time when she was to receive her bonus, the more dissatisfied she became. When Suzanne came to Vivian she was ready to leave her job because she felt that the amount she would earn in bonus was grossly unfair in light of what she had accomplished over the past year. Vivian suggested that she explain to her boss how she felt and, in light of her performance, ask him to adjust the amount of the bonus. Suzanne responded that she couldn't because of the way the bonus plan was structured. After a little coaching, she went to her boss and was able to negotiate a bigger bonus.

Suzanne was intimidated by what she understood "the rules" to be. Before talking with Vivian, she never even seriously considered trying to renegotiate her bonus. Instead, she was ready to leave a job she liked and did very well. Women are socialized as young girls to follow the rules. They are rewarded for respecting authority. They don't have a lot of role models to show them how to get around the rules. As a result, they are more likely to be intimidated by the invocation of "company policy." Unfortunately, to succeed in negotiations you sometimes need to figure out ways to get around the rules.

Another mistake women make is to be too deferential. From her years of experience placing women in high-level executive positions, Maxine Hartley concludes that "many women have a difficult time being direct when it comes to money, power, and titles. Women want these things as

much as men but frequently do not claim their right to them when negotiating." By placing too much importance on relationship building for
its own sake during the negotiating process, women often find it difficult to take firm negotiating positions. They agree in order to be liked,
whereas they would be more successful by firmly maintaining their
position. Men, on the other hand, are more likely to remain focused on
their goals. By the same token, a desire to avoid disagreements often
results in women finding creative solutions that satisfy everyone's
needs. (See Strategy 5—Creating a Win-Win Situation.) Some of the best
negotiators are women who are firm in their resolve to achieve certain
goals but flexible in how they go about achieving them.

Women also tend to be more sensitive than men to issues of fairness.
This can work to their advantage when negotiating compensation with
a new employer. However, it also can work to their disadvantage,
because it frequently results in their being too accommodating to the
positions taken by their adversary in the negotiations. Moreover, it is
particularly problematic when women are asking their current employers for more money. Typically women base their requests for higher
salaries on fairness rather than on their contribution to the organization.
When they ask for raises, they talk about issues of fairness such as how
many years they have been with the company, how they trained their
boss, and how their salary is less than Joe's. An appeal to fairness is
much less effective when you are negotiating with a current employer
than with a new company. (See How to Negotiate with Your Current
Employer.) It puts your superiors on the defensive. They are forced to
justify their previous actions. By agreeing to give you what you are
requesting, on the basis of an appeal to fairness, they would be admit-
ting that what they had done was wrong. After all, they are the ones
who are responsible for the actions that you are claiming to be unfair.
Therefore, instead of talking about fairness when seeking a raise,
emphasize your financial contribution to the organization.

Summary of Key Points

- There is no one right way for women to negotiate.
- Be yourself and develop your own negotiating style.
- Don't be afraid to ask for more than you think you can get.
- Don't feel overly encumbered by what you consider to be the "rules";
  sometimes you need to find a way to get around the rules.
- Try to avoid appeals to fairness when you are dealing with your cur-
  rent employer.

How to Negotiate with Your Current Employer

Regardless of what company you work for,
never forget the most important product
you're selling is yourself.

H. JACKSON BROWN

Many of the strategies discussed in this book apply or can be adapted to negotiating with your current employer. In order to use those strategies with your current employer, however, you need to recognize that the dynamics of that relationship are different from those that exist when you are negotiating with a new employer. Unfortunately, most companies tend to take their employees for granted. That is one reason executives who stay with the same company for a long time tend to fall behind their more mobile peers in terms of salary and benefits. By the same token, after being with one company for some period of time, employees get comfortable. They tend not to push as hard to improve their compensation as they do when they are changing jobs. Moreover, most significant increases in salary when you are already with a company result either from an increase in responsibilities, often in connection with a promotion, or from concerns that you might leave. Therefore, any strategy you use with your current employer should include an effort to get more responsibility or make yourself so invaluable that the possibility of your leaving would cause immediate concern.

When you are interviewing with a new company, you are always selling yourself. You need to do the same thing with your current employer, not just once a year at review time, but all year long. You need to constantly market yourself within your own company. Without appearing to be self-promoting, make sure key people throughout the company, especially your boss, know what you are accomplishing. Although we all assume that our bosses know what we are doing, the truth is that they usually have only the most general understanding of what their subordinates are working on.

Communication is critical. So is your communication style. Your boss needs to hear about every success. He or she should be kept abreast of your achievements, but in a way that does not appear to be bragging. Executive coaches teach their clients to work on developing a relationship with their boss which allows them just to call up or drop by and matter of factly deliver the news whenever something good happens. Linda Seale, a successful human resources executive and career coach in New York City, describes this as "practicing being casual." Executives who are good at their jobs and master this technique can rise meteorically. In fact, one executive coach tells the story of an executive who was able to use this technique to increase her annual salary from a little over $100,000 to almost $1 million in less than a year.

You should also send copies of relevant memos to people who have an interest in projects you are working on. Take the opportunity to discuss what you are doing with employees in other areas who might be affected by your work, particularly if they are at higher levels than you. Similarly you should show an interest in what others are working on, offering assistance where it is appropriate. Seek out high-visibility projects where you can showcase your talents. Remember, if others in the organization speak highly of you and want to work with you, your value will soar in the eyes of your boss and others in positions to influence your compensation.

The most important way to improve your negotiating position with your current employer is to do an outstanding job. Hard work and good results matter. However, they are not enough by themselves. You also need to convince your boss that you are important to the organization and would be difficult to replace. The best way to do that is to make your boss look good. (See Strategy 20—Making the Company Negotiator Look Good.)

We all tend to be motivated by self-interest. (See Strategy 8—Creating a Stake in the Outcome.) Your boss is probably no exception. When it comes time to decide on your raise or bonus, your boss is not likely to forget the things you did that made him or her shine in the eyes of others. Align your priorities with those of your boss. Don't ignore the other things you do that are important to the success of the organization, but make sure that you give priority to the projects your boss considers critical. If your boss needs something, make sure to deliver it promptly and make sure it is correct. You want to be viewed as someone who can be counted on when your boss needs something important done. Athletes call this the "go-to person"—that is, the person you want to get the ball to when you're in the final seconds of the game and need to score. Being that person for your boss will distinguish you from your co-workers.

It is also a good idea to share the credit for your successes with your boss. (In addition, always share credit with the people who work with you and for you, and who helped you achieve those successes. If you don't, your successes will no doubt be fewer, because those people will not continue to help you in the future.) The more you make your boss look good, the more he or she will fight for you when it comes time to determine salary increases. Attitude is also important. You are much more likely to get raises and promotions if you are enthusiastic and have a "can do" attitude. (See Strategy 9—Disagree Without Being Disagreeable: Being Likable as a Negotiating Strategy.)

Build a case all year long for increasing your salary. Don't start thinking about it shortly before your annual performance review is due. Keep a record of your accomplishments during the year. Two to three months before your annual review, find a way to outline for your boss what you have achieved during the past year. That is sufficient time prior to your review to have an impact on it. On the other hand, it is soon enough that it will not appear that you are trying directly to affect the outcome.

Another way to increase your salary is to seek out additional responsibilities. Be creative in suggesting additional areas for yourself. Equally important, recognize when opportunities arise to take on more responsibility and take advantage of them. I am reminded of one executive who did that with great results. Judith was executive vice president in charge of finance for a restaurant chain. When the president of the company abruptly resigned, she offered to take responsibility for several other departments. Although the position did not remain open long enough for her to establish herself as a contender for the president's job, when a new president was appointed she continued to supervise two of the departments that had temporarily reported to her. As a result, she was given a significant salary increase and awarded a substantial number of additional stock options.

You should also take every opportunity to learn new skills that are needed by the organization. Let people know that you have those skills and use them. By taking on additional responsibilities and learning new skills, you can make a case for being promoted. (See Strategy 4— Negotiate the Position, Not the Salary.) Doing so creates a "no lose" situation. If your case is strong enough, you may get the promotion you are seeking. With promotions come salary increases. If you are considered to be a valuable employee but a promotion is not forthcoming, you are still likely to get a sizable raise to assuage your feelings and to keep you from leaving. You can always revisit the issue of a promotion at a later date. Even if you believe that a promotion is not possible at this particular time, making your case for one will increase the probability of your getting a salary increase. (See Strategy 15—Creating Red Herring Issues.) That, of course, is your primary goal.

Timing is important as well. By properly timing your request for more money, you maximize the likelihood that you will be successful. (See Strategy 11—Patience, Persistence, and Timing: Outmaneuvering or Outlasting Your Opponent.) In many companies raises and bonuses are given out once a year in conjunction with annual performance reviews. In smaller companies raises tend to be given out on ad hoc basis. If salary increases occur at a set time each year, you need to keep that in mind; but you are not limited to seeking one only at that time. You are always free to sit down with your boss to discuss compensation. If you need an excuse to do so, you can always create one. (See Strategy 13— Using Another Offer Even When You Don't Have One.)

To the extent that you can control the timing of various projects you are working on, time the completion of high-visibility projects to coincide with your annual review. Most people have very short memories when it comes to the successes of others. Regardless of when it occurs, after you have achieved a major success is a good time to approach your boss to ask for additional responsibilities or more money. (See Strategy 22—Using Information: Facts, Figures and Comparisons.) Particularly if your work has had a significant impact on the company's bottom line, you may be in a position to seek a raise outside the normal review cycle. Even if you aren't given a raise at that time, you will no doubt be told that what you have accomplished will be taken into account at review time. You will be able to remind your boss of that promise prior to your next review. If you have the choice between asking for more money or asking for additional responsibilities, it is usually best to seek the latter. Your request will be better received and a salary increase will likely follow once you are given added responsibility.

When you are dealing with your current employer, you also need to be aware of your market value. You should test the waters in the job market frequently. Stay visible in your industry. Play an active role in trade associations. Go out of your way to meet and get to know executive recruiters, particularly when you are not looking for a job. Always return their phone calls. If you are not interested in a search they are handling, help them identify potential candidates. That way they will be sure to call you the next time they have a search in which you might have an interest. Constantly market yourself, both inside and outside your company. Talk to any company that shows an interest in you, provided you can do so without your current employer finding out. Determine how marketable you are and what you could earn elsewhere. Then use that information to get your employer to increase your salary. (See Strategy 13—Using Another Offer Even When You Don't Have One.) If you have a realistic understanding of how marketable you are and the salary you can command, you will be confident in your arguments when you seek a salary increase.

By the same token, you should try to determine what the company is paying new hires. (See Getting Ready to Negotiate.) The fact that a company has to pay higher salaries to recruit from the outside can be used to show that your salary has gotten out of line with the market. Use it to support other data showing that your salary is no longer competitive. As previously discussed, comparing your salary with others in the organization is less likely to be effective, since those salaries have been set by the company. Attacking their fairness will be viewed as an attack on the company. By raising the issue in that way, you may actually reduce the likelihood that your salary will be adjusted, because the company may feel a need to justify its earlier salary decisions. (See Gender Differences in Negotiating.)

Getting your current employer to increase your compensation is an ongoing process. You are continuously setting the stage on the basis of your job performance and how you market yourself. Much of what would be done through the give-and-take of negotiations with a new employer is done with your current employer through regular communications about your achievements. Your current employer will ordinarily determine the amount of any regular salary increase on the basis of your prior year's increase, adjusted for changes in the general level of companywide increases and for changes in the level of your performance or responsibility. If you want to exceed that formula, you need to build a case over the course of the year as to why you should get more. You need to show that you have achieved results well above the norm, that you have taken on additional responsibilities or that your value in the market is higher than previously recognized. Once you build your case, you may not have to do anything further to get the salary increase you deserve. (See Strategy 23—Silence Is Golden: When to Let the Other Side Talk.) Alternatively, you may want to actively seek your boss's help in getting your salary adjusted. (See Strategy 14—Not Negotiating as a

Strategy.) In the event that, despite your efforts, the company still fails to recognize your true market value, you may have to change jobs in order to get the compensation you are capable of commanding in the market. (See Strategy 25—Walking Away.)

Summary of Negotiating Points

- Recognize that the dynamics of an ongoing employment relationship are different from the dynamics of negotiating with a new employer.

- Continuously market yourself both inside and outside the company.

- Make your boss look good.

- Share credit for your successes.

- Communicate your successes to your boss on a regular basis.

- Several months before your annual review, find a way to outline for your boss what you have accomplished during the past year.

- Learn new skills that are needed by the organization.

- Seek out additional responsibilities.

- Be aware of your market value.

- If the company fails to recognize your true market value despite your best efforts, you may want to explore the possibility of changing employers.

When You're Unemployed: How to Gain Bargaining Leverage Even If You Think You Have None

*The greatest discovery of my generation is
that a human being can alter his life by
altering his attitudes.*   WILLIAM JAMES

Frank came to me for advice. He had been unemployed for almost three months. He didn't have a job offer yet. He was talking to several companies and wanted to be prepared in the event one of the them decided to make him an offer. We talked and got to know each other. Frank was a marketing executive with an impressive background. He had lost his position following a takeover. He was looking for a marketing position at a company where he could possibly one day become president.

Frank was optimistic that any day he would get an offer. Over the next few weeks I spoke to Frank periodically to find out how things were going. Every time we talked, he told me about the companies he was meeting with. Finally, after several months, he got an offer from a company in Boston. The offer was a good one. Nonetheless, we did our research and developed a negotiating strategy focused on getting additional equity and a commitment to being promoted to a bigger job if he did well.

Frank did not rush the negotiations. While we were negotiating, Frank continued to meet with other companies. In fact, shortly thereafter he received another offer. In the end, we were able to get everything we wanted from the company in Boston and he accepted that job.

Despite the fact that finding a job took longer than he expected, Frank exuded confidence throughout. I know there were times that privately he must have wondered whether he would ever again have a job as good as the one he just left. Nonetheless, he didn't panic. He never showed doubts—not to me, and certainly not to any prospective employers. As a result, Frank ended up with two very good job offers and was able to negotiate an excellent deal.

During my career I have known many people who had to endure a period of unemployment—some of them were friends, some were clients, and some were people whom I personally had to lay off from their jobs. Being unemployed is always a difficult time, not only for the person without a job but for his or her family as well. The good news is that all of them found jobs that they liked at least as much as the ones they left. Although being unemployed is unsettling, with the benefit of hindsight and a new job, these employees are glad they were forced to go through the process. Being laid off required them to examine who they were and what they wanted to do with the rest of their lives. Almost all of them are much happier in their new jobs and are excited by the fresh challenges they face daily. Having grown comfortable in their jobs and with families to support, few of them would have considered leaving on their own to try something else.

Because of the large number of mergers, acquisitions, and downsizings that have occurred in recent years, being unemployed no longer has the stigma that it once did. Employers know that good employees lose their jobs through no fault of their own. In fact, one well-known executive recruiter told me that her ideal candidate is no longer someone who has been with one company for an entire career. Today, the successful executive is one who can handle change well. Executives who have worked at different companies are often better able to adapt. Employers and executive recruiters understand that.

In the context of employment negotiations, the only difference between a candidate who is employed and a candidate who is unemployed is often confidence. If you believe in yourself and exhibit that confidence to the world, you will be able to employ all the strategies discussed in this book just as if you were employed. Of course, you still need to prepare thoroughly and be able to recognize when a particular strategy is appropriate. But how you negotiate when you are unemployed is mainly a matter of attitude.

Frank is good example. Throughout his job search he maintained a positive attitude. He was confident that he was going to be able to find a good job. He pursued his job search aggressively and treated it just as he would any other marketing campaign. He even came to me in advance of having received a job offer so that he would be prepared when one came. He continued to exhibit that confidence even though the search took longer than he expected. As long as you maintain a positive attitude, you will be able to negotiate from a position of strength. Not only will you be able to negotiate better, but you will find that employers are more interested in hiring you.

Sometimes an employer thinks you will take less money because you are unemployed. You need to convey, by the way you present yourself, that this is not the case. If you allow employers to believe that, you not only will get less money but you will make yourself less attractive as a candidate as well. All employers think they are special and that you should want to work for them. Employers are not looking for candidates who take the job only because they can't find anything else. They are looking for people who really want to work for the company and who won't leave as soon as something better comes along. As Ted Pilonero, a well-known New York human resources consultant, pointed out: "If people act like they are desperate for a job, most employers will immediately lose interest." Never allow an employer to believe you don't have other options. If you are hired on that basis, you will be taken for granted throughout your career with the company.

If all else fails, you can always turn down the job offer, leaving the door open for the company to improve upon it. (See Strategy 25—Walking Away.) Obviously you would do so only when other strategies have failed and you are not willing to accept the job on the terms being offered. Under those circumstances, turning down the offer can be used to strengthen your bargaining position with other employers. You can strategically let other prospective employers know about the offer and that you turned it down.

How do you stay positive when you are unemployed? It is easy to get discouraged. There are, however, several things you can do. First and foremost, take good care of yourself physically. Exercise regularly. Watch what you eat. Dress well. Buy some new clothes. The better you look and feel, the more confident you will be.

You should also get into a routine: exercise; make a certain number of calls each day to people who might be helpful with your job search; meet with those individuals who are willing to meet with you; send follow-up letters; and then plan your next day's activity. The busier you are, the better.

The best way to strengthen your negotiating position is to have options. (See Strategy 13—Using Another Offer Even When You Don't Have One.) Human nature is such that if you have two job offers you will almost always bargain harder, because if one deal doesn't work out you always have the other to fall back on. Psychologically you tend to behave the same way if you are talking with a number of other employers, even if you don't actually have another offer. That is why Frank kept meeting with other potential employers even though he was seriously negotiating with one company.

Probably the most important thing you can do to remain confident throughout the difficult period of unemployment is to find someone you can talk to about what you are doing and how you feel. A spouse or significant other can serve this purpose, but it is usually better to find someone who is less personally involved and who understands what you are going through. An outplacement counselor or career coach will serve that purpose nicely. As part of any severance package, it is usually a good idea to try to get your employer to pay for outplacement. There are a number of support groups made up of people who are also unemployed. These groups meet regularly so that their members can help one another with their searches, share information, and provide moral support. Some are affiliated with outplacement services; others can be found through church or community organizations. Ask people who have recently gone through the process.

There will be times when you get down and things appear hopeless. Just knowing that there are other people going through the same process and experiencing the same feelings can help you maintain a good attitude. Often you will be able to keep things in perspective when you compare yourself with others who are worse off. In addition, every time a member of the group finds a job, it tends to renew your faith that things eventually will turn out well. Those people will continue to be helpful to you in your job search as well. They may also be helpful to you later on in your career. Most important, some of them will become your friends.

Whether you are employed or unemployed, if you have the right attitude, you will be able to use the techniques described in this book to negotiate with a new employer effectively. You will be able to start your new career knowing that you have negotiated the best possible deal. From there, if you perform well, you should be able to continue to use what you have learned to improve upon it.

Summary of Negotiating Points

- Always maintain a positive attitude.
- Demonstrate to the world that you have confidence in yourself and your abilities.
- Take pride in your appearance. Exercise regularly and dress well.
- Find a disinterested person you can talk to about what you are going through; join a support group.
- Actively conduct your job search so that, even if you're negotiating with one company, you always have other potential opportunities in the works.
- Remember that many others have gone through what you are going through and ended up much better off than they were before.

About the Author

Lee E. Miller is Senior Vice President of Human Resources for Barneys New York, one of the premier specialty retailers in the nation. He is also an Adjunct Professor at the Seton Hall University's Stillman School of Business, where he teaches in the MBA program. Previously, he was a partner and head of the employment and labor group of one of the largest law firms in New Jersey. He also worked as a Vice President of Human Resources at R.H. Macy & Co., Inc. and as a consultant for Advanced Human Resources Group Inc.

Mr. Miller is a graduate of Harvard Law School. He has extensive experience in negotiating employment agreements on behalf of executives and corporations. Among the clients he has represented are the National Football League Management Council, The United States Golf Association, American Express, Lafayette College and the chairmen, presidents, and senior executives of several Fortune 1000 companies. He is the former Chairman of the Committee on Employment Law of the New York Chapter of the American Corporate Counsel Association, a member of the National Retail Federation's Committee on Employment Law and a member of the American Bar Association Committee on Individual Rights and Responsibilities.

He has taught negotiating tactics to senior executives receiving outplacement at Right Associates, one of the largest outplacement firms in the country. He frequently addresses groups, such as the Wall Street Employment Managers Association. Exec-U-Net and the Association of Women Financial Executives, on how to negotiate employment agreements.

Index